QuarkXPress® 3.1 Quick Reference

Barbara Assadi

QuarkXPress 3.1 Quick Reference.

Copyright ©1992 by Que Corporation.

All rights reserved. Printed in the United States of America. No part of this book may be used or reproduced in any form or by any means, or stored in a database or retrieval system, without prior written permission of the publisher except in the case of brief quotations embodied in critical articles and reviews. Making copies of any part of this book for any purpose other than your own personal use is a violation of United States copyright laws. For information, address Que Corporation, 11711 North College Avenue, Suite 140, Carmel, IN 46032.

Library of Congress Catalog Number: 91-62310

ISBN: 0-88022-769-9

This book is sold *as is*, without warranty of any kind, either express or implied, respecting the contents of this book, including but not limited to implied warranties for the book's quality, performance, merchantability, or fitness for any particular purpose. Neither Que Corporation nor its dealers or distributors shall be liable to the purchaser or any other person or entity with respect to any liability, loss, or damage caused or alleged to be caused directly or indirectly by this book.

95 94 93 92   4 3 2 1

Interpretation of the printing code: the rightmost double-digit number is the year of the book's printing; the rightmost single-digit number is the number of the book's printing. For example, a printing code of 92-1 shows that the first printing of the book occurred in 1992.

This book is based on QuarkXPress Version 3.1.

Que Quick Reference Series

The *Que Quick Reference Series* is a portable resource of essential microcomputer knowledge. Drawing on the experience of many of Que's best-selling authors, this series helps you easily access important program information. The *Que Quick Reference Series* includes these titles:

1-2-3 for DOS Release 2.3 Quick Reference
1-2-3 for DOS Release 3.1+ Quick Reference
1-2-3 for Windows Quick Reference
1-2-3 Release 2.2 Quick Reference
Allways Quick Reference
AutoCAD Quick Reference, 2nd Edition
Batch Files and Macros Quick Reference
CheckFree Quick Reference
CorelDRAW! Quick Reference
dBASE IV Quick Reference
Excel for Windows Quick Reference
Fastback Quick Reference
Hard Disk Quick Reference
Harvard Graphics Quick Reference
LapLink Quick Reference
Microsoft Word 5 Quick Reference
Microsoft Word Quick Reference
Microsoft Works Quick Reference
MS-DOS 5 Quick Reference
MS-DOS Quick Reference
Norton Utilities Quick Reference
Paradox 3.5 Quick Reference
PC Tools 7 Quick Reference
Q&A 4 Quick Reference
QuarkXPress 3.1 Quick Reference
Quattro Pro Quick Reference
Quicken Quick Reference
System 7 Quick Reference
UNIX Programmer's Quick Reference
UNIX Shell Commands Quick Reference
Windows 3 Quick Reference
WordPerfect 5.1 Quick Reference
WordPerfect for Windows Quick Reference
WordPerfect Quick Reference

Publisher
>Lloyd J. Short

Production Editor
>Laura J. Wirthlin

Technical Editor
>Eric Diamond

Production Team
>Betty Kish, Bob LaRoche, Laurie Lee,
>Johnna VanHoose

Trademark Acknowledgments
>Apple, ImageWriter, and LaserWriter are registered trademarks of Apple Computer, Inc. EPS and PostScript are registered trademarks of Adobe Systems Incorporated. FreeHand is a registered trademark of Aldus Corporation. Geneva is a trademark of Epson America, Inc. Helvetica and Times are registered trademarks of Linotype-Hell Co. Mac3D is a registered trademark of Challenger Software Corporation. MacWrite is a registered trademark and MacDraw is a trademark of Claris Corporation. Microsoft, Microsoft Word, Microsoft Works, and Microsoft Write are registered trademarks of Microsoft Corporation. PANTONE is a registered trademark of PANTONE, Inc. QuarkXPress is a registered trademark of Quark, Inc. SuperPaint is a trademark of Silicon Beach Software, Inc. WordPerfect is a registered trademark of WordPerfect Corporation.

Table of Contents

Introduction ix

HINTS FOR USING THIS BOOK 1

QUARKXPRESS BASICS 2
The Mouse 2
Menus 3
Dialog Boxes 4
Palettes 5
Document Windows 8

COMMAND REFERENCE 9
Alignment 9
Anchored Rules 10
Anchored Lines and Boxes 12
Append 13
Application Preferences 14
Apply 16
Baseline Grid 17
Baseline Shift 18
Bleeds 18
Boxes 19
Check Spelling 21
Colors 23
Columns 27
Constraining 28
Continued on (from) 29
Copy 30
Default Settings 30

Deleting	33
Duplicating Items	36
Exporting Text	37
Find/Change	37
Font Handling	42
Font Usage	46
Frames	47
General Preferences	49
Get Picture	51
Get Text	53
Greeking	54
Groups	55
Guides and Rulers	56
Halftone Screens	58
Help	60
Hyphenation and Justification	61
Indents	64
Initial Caps	65
Kerning	67
Keyboard Shortcuts	70
Leading	78
Libraries	79
Lines	82
Linking	86
Locked Lines and Boxes	87
Margin Guides	88
Master Pages	89
Measurements Palette	92
Modifying Items	93
Moving Items	97
Opening and Closing Documents	99

Page Numbering	100
Page Setup	102
Page Size	105
Paragraph Formats	106
PICT Files	108
Picture Color	108
Picture Contrast	109
Printing	112
Process Color	114
Registration Marks	115
Resizing	116
Rotating	117
Runaround	118
Service Bureaus	119
Skewing	120
Space/Align	120
Special Characters	121
Spot Color	123
Spreads	124
Suppress Printout	126
Tabs	127
Templates	128
Thumbnails	129
TIFF/RIFF Files	130
Tiling	132
Tool Palette	132
Tool Preferences	133
Tracking	135
Trapping	136
Typesetter's Punctuation	138
Typographic Preferences	139

Views 141
Word Processing 142
XPress Tags 142
Xtensions 144

Index **145**

Introduction

QuarkXPress 3.1 Quick Reference includes the quick reference information you need to use QuarkXPress. This book offers step-by-step explanations of how to use QuarkXPress and, wherever possible, includes suggestions on keyboard shortcuts you can use as your proficiency with QuarkXPress grows.

QuarkXPress 3.1 Quick Reference is not meant to replace the documentation included with QuarkXPress. Instead, this book highlights the features you are most likely to use in developing a QuarkXPress document. For example, the program's documentation includes several pages of XPress Tags, which are QuarkXPress's character-formatting tags. This book lists just a few of the most common XPress Tags and explains how you can use them.

The Command Reference is an alphabetical listing of QuarkXPress tasks and topics. The *Get Text* entry, for example, tells you how to import text created in a word processing application into QuarkXPress. Another entry, *Xtensions*, tells you how to find out about third-party software modules that add additional capabilities to QuarkXPress.

Now you have essential information at your fingertips with *QuarkXPress 3.1 Quick Reference*—and the entire *Que Quick Reference Series*.

x

HINTS FOR USING THIS BOOK

QuarkXPress 3.1 Quick Reference has two main sections.

QuarkXPress Basics provides information about the QuarkXPress interface that you need to know in order to use the Command Reference effectively.

The Command Reference is an alphabetical listing of QuarkXPress commands and features. Each entry includes the purpose of the command or feature and step-by-step instructions for its use. Some entries also include instructions for performing a task in more than one way. The keyboard method explains how to perform the task by using a series of keystrokes. The Measurements palette method explains how to perform the task by using the Measurements palette.

Conventions used in this book

As you read this book, keep in mind the following conventions:

- The keys you press and text you type appear in **boldface blue** type. In this book, the text you type appears in UPPERCASE, but you can use upper- or lowercase.

- To use key combinations, hold down the first key, such as the **Command** (⌘) or **Shift** key, as you press the second key. The following is a typical entry:

    To center the paragraph, press **⌘-Shift-C**.

- All on-screen messages appear in a `special` typeface. The following is a typical entry:

    `No similar words found`

- The information in this book is extensively cross-referenced. For more information about a feature, turn to the entry referenced in *italic* type. The following is a typical entry:

    See also *Alignment*.

Hints for Using This Book

QUARKXPRESS BASICS

QuarkXPress is a powerful desktop publishing program. The program enables you to merge text and graphics files created in other applications and to lay out the pages of the resulting document using the features of QuarkXPress. The program also enables you to create a document from beginning to end, entering text within QuarkXPress and using the program's integrated drawing tools to add simple graphics.

What distinguishes QuarkXPress from its competitors is the amazing degree of control the program offers over every aspect of a document page. For example, you can rotate text and graphic boxes not just one degree at a time, but also in increments of .001 degree. You can specify type sizes from 2 to 720 points in increments of .001 of any measurement unit. Virtually every QuarkXPress function offers equally impressive control.

The Mouse

You use the mouse to navigate the QuarkXPress screen and to select items.

To click an item

Position the mouse pointer on the item, and then press and release the mouse button.

To double-click an item

Position the mouse pointer on the item, and then click the mouse button twice in rapid succession.

To drag an item

Position the mouse pointer on the item. Press and hold down the mouse button, and then slide the mouse across a flat surface to move the item to a different location.

Menus

Menus are lists of related QuarkXPress commands. The menu names appear in the *menu bar* at the top of the screen.

To select a menu

Position the mouse pointer on the menu name and press the mouse button. The menu remains selected until you release the mouse button.

To select a menu command

1. Select the menu that contains the command you want to select.

2. Drag the mouse pointer down the list of commands to highlight the command you want to use.

3. Release the mouse button.

   QuarkXPress executes that command or displays a submenu or dialog box from which you make additional selections.

   When you select a command that is followed by a *submenu indicator* (a triangle at the right side of the menu), QuarkXPress displays an additional menu, or *submenu*, of selections related to the main menu item.

   When you select a command that is followed by an ellipsis (...), QuarkXPress displays a *dialog box*.

To select a submenu option

1. From the menu command that displays the submenu, drag the mouse pointer to the right, highlighting the first option in the submenu.

2. Drag the mouse pointer down the list of options to highlight the option you want to use.

3. Release the mouse button.

   QuarkXPress executes that command and option.

Dialog Boxes

When you select a menu command followed by an ellipsis (...), QuarkXPress displays a *dialog box*. Certain other commands, such as Find/Change, also produce a dialog box.

Dialog boxes contain *fields* (where you enter values), *pop-up menus* (from which you select options in the same way you select commands from other menus), and *check boxes* and *option* and *command buttons* (which you click to indicate selections).

Pop-up menus

When you make a selection in a dialog box or palette, you may have access to a *pop-up menu*.

To select an option from a pop-up menu, drag the mouse pointer down the menu to highlight the option you want to use, and then release the mouse button.

Check boxes

Many dialog boxes contain options that have a small square *check box*. (Usually the check box appears to the left of the option.)

If the check box has an X in it, that option is *selected* and applies to the corresponding item in the document. If the check box is empty, that option is not selected.

To select or deselect a check box, position the mouse pointer in the box and click the mouse button.

Option buttons

Many dialog boxes contain sets of options that have small round *option buttons*. (Usually the option button appears to the left of the option.)

If the option button has a black dot in it, that option is *selected* and applies to the corresponding item in the document. If the option button is empty, that option is not selected.

To select or deselect an option button, position the mouse pointer in the button and click the mouse button. You can select only one option button in each set.

Command buttons

Many dialog boxes also have *command buttons*, which execute a command such as OK or Cancel. Command buttons usually appear near the bottom of the dialog box.

To select a command button, position the mouse pointer in the button and click the mouse button. The default command button has a bold line around it. You also can select the default button by pressing Enter.

Palettes

QuarkXPress also has *palettes*, free-standing windows containing additional selections that perform a wide range of functions.

Document Layout palette

The Document Layout palette appears on-screen when you select the Show Document Layout command from the View menu.

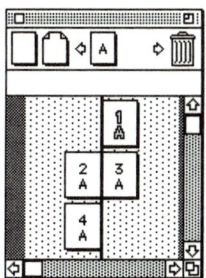

QuarkXPress Basics

Library palette

The Library palette appears on-screen when you select the Library command from the Utilities menu.

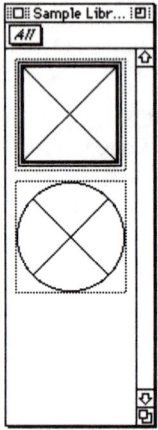

Measurements palette

The Measurements palette appears on-screen when you select the Show Measurements command from the View menu. The Measurements palette varies somewhat according to the active item.

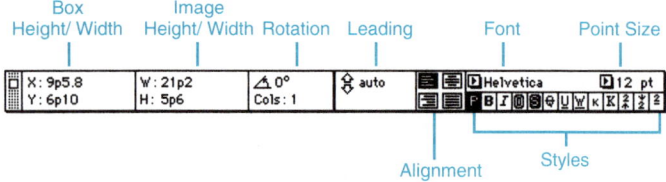

Tool palette

The Tool palette usually appears on the left side of the document window, but you can drag it to a different position.

The following list describes the tools in the order they appear on the Tool palette.

Tool	Name	Use
	Item	Moving, grouping and ungrouping, cutting, copying, and pasting text boxes, picture boxes, lines, and groups.
	Content	Importing text and graphics and editing, cutting, copying, pasting, and changing the contents of text and picture boxes.
	Rotation	Rotating items manually.
	Zoom	Enlarging or reducing the dimensions of the window's contents.
	Text Box	Drawing text boxes.
	Rectangular Picture Box	Drawing rectangular picture boxes.
	Rounded-Corner Rectangular Picture Box	Drawing rectangular picture boxes with rounded corners.
	Oval Picture Box	Drawing oval and circular picture boxes.
	Polygon Picture Box	Drawing free-form polygonal picture boxes with three or more sides.
	Orthogonal Line	Drawing vertical and horizontal lines.
	Line	Drawing lines at any angle.
	Linking	Creating links between text boxes so that text can flow from one text box to another.
	Unlinking	Breaking links between text boxes.

QuarkXPress Basics

Document Windows

A *document window* is the screen display of an open QuarkXPress document.

Picture boxes

Picture boxes are boxes that can contain pictures. Picture boxes have attributes that determine the position, size, and color of the pictures they contain.

To activate (select) a picture box, click the mouse button anywhere inside the picture box.

Text boxes

Text boxes are boxes that can contain text. Text boxes have attributes that determine the position, size, color, columns, and text inset of the text they contain.

To activate (select) a text box, click the mouse button anywhere inside the text box.

To select (highlight) text

1. Select the **Content** tool.

2. Click and hold down the mouse button at the beginning of the text you want to select.

3. Drag the mouse to the end of the passage you want to select.

    The program selects and highlights the text.

4. Release the mouse button.

To activate an item

Select the **Item** tool or **Content** tool (depending on the situation), then click the item you want to activate. When you activate an item, the program displays small black boxes, or *handles*, at its sides and corners.

To create, open, or close a document

See *Opening and Closing Documents* in the Command Reference.

COMMAND REFERENCE

The Command Reference is an alphabetical listing of the commands and features of QuarkXPress. Each entry includes the purpose of the command or feature and step-by-step instructions for its use.

Alignment

Purpose

Aligns or justifies paragraphs horizontally or vertically.

To align or justify paragraphs horizontally

1. Select the Content tool. (If you are changing the alignment for a specific paragraph, the Content tool is selected already.)

2. Activate the text box for which you want to align all the paragraphs.

   or

   Position the insertion bar anywhere within the individual paragraph for which you want to change the default alignment.

3. From the Style menu, select Alignment. From the Alignment submenu, select Left, Center, Right, or Justify.

Keyboard method

1. Select the Content tool and activate the text box that contains the paragraph you want to align.

2. To align the paragraph to the left, press ⌘-Shift-L.

   To center the paragraph, press ⌘-Shift-C.

   To align the paragraph to the right, press ⌘-Shift-R.

   To justify the paragraph horizontally, press ⌘-Shift-J.

Measurements palette method

1. Select the Content tool and activate the text box that contains the paragraph you want to align.

2. Click the appropriate Measurements palette alignment icon. For more information, see *Palettes* in the QuarkXPress Basics section.

3. Press Enter.

To align or justify paragraphs vertically

1. Activate the text box you want to align or justify vertically.

2. From the Item menu, select Modify.

   The program displays the Text Box Specifications dialog box.

3. From the Type pop-up menu, select Top, Centered, Bottom, or Justified. If you select Justified, enter the maximum space between paragraphs in the Inter Paragraph Max field. To distribute the space between lines and paragraphs evenly, enter 0.

Anchored Rules

Purpose

Anchored rules are lines attached to the top or bottom of a paragraph. When you move the text, any anchored rules also move.

To place an anchored rule

1. Select the Content tool and activate the text box that contains or will contain the paragraph(s) to which you want to attach anchored rules.

2. From the Style menu, select Rules (or press ⌘-Shift-N).

   The program displays the Paragraph Rules dialog box. Selections you make in the Paragraph Rules dialog box apply only to active text boxes that do not yet contain text (affecting all paragraphs you enter until you change to different paragraph rules) or to selected paragraphs.

3. Select the Rule Above or Rule Below check box.

   The program displays a dialog box where you can specify the length, offset, style, width, color, and shade of the rule. If you select both the Rule Above and Rule Below check boxes, the dialog box expands to display selection fields for each type of rule.

4. To extend the rule from the paragraph's left indent to its right indent, select Indents from the Length pop-up menu. To specify the distance between the left (or right) ends of a rule and the paragraph's left (or right) indent, enter a value in the From Left (or From Right) field. A positive value extends the rule beyond the indents; a negative value indents the rule between the indents.

   To make the rule the same length as the first line of text (for Rule Above) or the last line of text (for Rule Below), select Text from the Length pop-up menu. To specify the distance between the left (or right) end of the rule and the end of the paragraph's first (or last) line of text, enter a value in the From Left (or From Right) field. A positive value extends the rule beyond the line; a negative value indents the rule between the ends of the line.

5. To control the distance between the paragraph and the rule, enter an offset (a specific value or a percentage of the default offset) in the Offset field.

6. To vary the style or width of the rule, select an option from the Style or Width pop-up menus or enter a value in the Width field.

7. To specify a color or shade for the rule, select an option from the Color or Shade pop-up menus. You can apply any color defined in the color palette.

8. To preview the paragraph rules without saving the changes, click the Apply button (or press ⌘-A).

9. To save the changes, click the OK button.

Anchored Lines and Boxes

Purpose

Anchors a line or box inside a text box. When you anchor an item, the item remains in the same position within the text box regardless of any edits you make to the rest of the document.

To anchor a line or box to text

1. Select the Item tool and activate the line or the text box or picture box you want to anchor to text.

2. From the Edit menu, select Cut (or press ⌘-X) or Copy (or press ⌘-C).

3. Select the Content tool and position the insertion bar in the text where you want to anchor the item. (If you do not use the Content tool for this step, you are not anchoring the item.)

4. From the Edit menu, select Paste (or press ⌘-V).

To modify an anchored box

1. Select the Item tool and activate the text box or picture box you want to modify.

2. From the Item menu, select Modify.

   The program displays the Anchored Text Box Specifications or Anchored Picture Box Specifications dialog box.

3. In the Align with Text area, select Ascent to align the anchored box to the top of uppercase text or select Baseline to align the anchored box to the baseline of the text.

4. To control the width and height of the box, enter dimensions in the Width and Height fields.

You also can size the box by entering dimensions in the W and H fields in the Measurements Palette.

To move an anchored box

1. Select the Content tool and activate the text box or picture box you want to move.

QuarkXPress 3.1 Quick Reference

2. From the Edit menu, select Cut (or press ⌘-**X**).

3. Position the insertion bar in the text where you want to place the anchored box.

4. From the Edit menu, select Paste (or press ⌘-**V**).

To use an anchored box as a drop cap

See *Initial Caps*.

Append

Purpose

Copies a set of specifications or a color from one document to another.

To add a style from a QuarkXPress or Microsoft Word document to the active document

To append a Microsoft Word style, the Microsoft Word filter must be in the QuarkXPress folder.

1. From the Edit menu, select Style Sheets.

   The program displays the Style Sheets dialog box.

2. In the dialog box, select Append.

   The program displays a scroll box.

3. Select the document that contains the style you want to add to the active document's available style sheets.

4. Click the Open button.

   The program displays the Style Sheets for *documentname* dialog box.

5. Select the style you want to append.

6. Click the Append button.

To add a color from a QuarkXPress document to the active document's color palette

1. From the Edit menu, select Colors.

   The program displays the Colors dialog box.

2. In the dialog box, select Append.

   The program displays a scroll box.

3. Select the document that contains the color you want to add to the active document's color palette.

4. Click the Open button.

   The program displays the colors for *documentname* dialog box.

5. In the dialog box, select the color you want to append.

6. Click the Append button.

Application Preferences

Purpose

Application preferences are programwide defaults that apply to *all* documents.

To define application preferences

1. From the Edit menu, select Preferences. From the Preferences submenu, select Application.

   The program displays the Application Preferences dialog box.

2. In the Guide Colors area, which controls the color of margin guides, ruler guides, and grid lines displayed on color monitors, select one or more of the following options:

   To change the color of margin guides, click the Margin button. The program displays the Margin Guide Color dialog box.

   To change the color of ruler guides, click the Ruler button. The program displays the Ruler Guide Color dialog box.

   To change the color of grids, click the Grid button. The program displays the Grid Color dialog box.

Use the color wheel and the fields in the dialog box to select the new color. For more information, see *Colors*.

3. In the Trap area, which controls how the program performs trapping, select the Auto Method, Auto Amount, Indeterminate, Overprint Limit, and Ignore White preferences. For more information, see *Trapping*.

4. In the Pasteboard Width field, specify the width (from 0 to 100 percent of the page width) of the pasteboard on either side of a spread or page. The default Pasteboard Width is 100 percent.

5. In the Reg. Marks Offset field, specify the distance from the edge of a page (from 0 to 30 points) that the program prints registration marks when you select Registration Marks in the Print dialog box. (To display this dialog box, select Print from the File menu.)

6. To update the document view as you drag scroll boxes in the document window's scroll bars, select the Live Scroll check box.

7. To enable scrolling in any direction (when you hold down the **Option** key as you drag the page with the Page Grabber Hand pointer), select the Page Grabber Hand check box.

8. To redraw the entire screen at one time rather than in sections, select the Off-screen Draw check box.

9. To save changes to a library each time you add an entry, select the Auto Library Save check box.

10. To lower the default resolution for displaying imported TIFF and RIFF pictures (from 72 dpi to 36 dpi), select the Low Resolution TIFF check box.

11. To display imported grayscale picture in 256 gray levels, select the 256 Levels of Gray check box. For this selection to be fully effective, you must have a monitor that can display 256 gray levels, and you must have scanned the imported picture with 256 gray levels.

12. To update the display of PANTONE Colors used in a document to match those in the PANTONE Selector, select the Calibrated PANTONE check box.

13. To save these Preferences, click the OK button.

Note

See also *Default Settings*, *General Preferences*, *Tool Preferences*, and *Typographic Preferences*.

Apply

Purpose

Enables you to see the effects of your dialog box selections without saving the changes. Continuous Apply mode enables you to make multiple selections in the dialog box, viewing the effect as you make each selection.

To use the Apply feature

1. In a dialog box that has an Apply button, select an option you want to preview.

2. Click the Apply button (or press ⌘-A) to view the effects of your dialog box selections.

3. To accept the selection, click the OK button.

4. To save the selection, select Save from the File menu (or press ⌘-S).

To use Continuous Apply mode

1. In a dialog box that has an Apply button, press ⌘-Option-A to view the effects of your dialog box selections continuously.

2. Select the options you want to preview.

3. To turn off the Continuous Apply mode, press ⌘-Option-A.

4. To accept the selections, click the OK button.

5. To undo the last change in the sequence of Continuous Apply selections, press ⌘-Z.

6. To save the selections, select Save from the File menu (or press ⌘-S).

Baseline Grid

Purpose

Provides a *baseline grid*, to which you can lock the baselines of text within paragraphs.

To set up the nonprinting baseline grid

1. From the Edit menu, select Preferences. From the Preferences submenu, select Typographic.

    The program displays the Typographic Preferences dialog box.

2. In the Start field (in the Baseline Grid area), enter the distance between the first line of the grid and the top of the page. The default Start value is 0.5 inches.

3. In the Increment field, enter the interval (from 5 to 144 points in .001-point increments) between grid baselines. The default Increment value is 12 points.

4. Click the OK button.

To lock text baselines to the baseline grid

1. From the Style menu, select Formats (or press ⌘-Shift-F).

    The program displays the Paragraph Formats dialog box.

2. To lock or unlock the lines of text in selected paragraphs to the document's baseline grid, select or deselect the Lock to Baseline Grid check box.

3. Click the OK button.

Baseline Shift

Purpose

Shifts characters the specified number of points above or below the baseline (the invisible line on which the type sits).

To shift characters above or below the baseline

1. Highlight the character or group of characters you want to shift above or below the baseline.

2. From the Style menu, select Baseline Shift.

    The program displays the Baseline Shift dialog box with the Baseline Shift field highlighted.

3. Enter a positive number to shift the characters above the baseline or a negative number to shift the characters below the baseline.

4. Click the OK button.

Keyboard method

1. Highlight the character or group of characters you want to shift above or below the baseline.

2. Press ⌘-**Option-Shift-+** to shift the characters above the baseline in 1-point increments.

    Press ⌘-**Option-Shift-hyphen** to shift the characters below the baseline in 1-point increments.

Bleeds

Purpose

Enables you to extend an illustration to the trimmed edge of a finished page or to an adjacent page.

To bleed a picture past the edge of a page

1. Activate the picture box that contains the illustration you want to bleed.

2. Drag the picture box beyond the edge of the page, onto the adjacent page in the layout or onto the pasteboard.

To print a page that has a bleed

   1. From the File menu, select Print.

      The program displays the Print dialog box.

   2. Select the Registration Marks check box.

   3. Print the page on paper that is slightly larger than the QuarkXPress page size so that the registration marks appear. (You set the page size in the New dialog box when you created the document.)

      or

      To proof the document, you can print the pages in a reduced size.

Boxes

Purpose

Holds pictures you import from other applications and text you import from other applications or enter using QuarkXPress's word processor.

To create a picture box

   1. Select one of the picture box tools (**Rectangular Picture Box**, **Rounded-Corner Rectangular Picture Box**, **Oval Picture Box**, or **Polygon Picture Box**) from the Tool palette.

   2. Position the picture box tool on the page where you want to place the picture.

   3. If you selected the **Rectangular Picture Box** tool, the **Rounded-Corner Rectangular Picture Box** tool, or the **Oval Picture Box** tool, click the mouse button and drag the cross hair (+) pointer to create the box to size.

If you selected the **Polygon Picture Box** tool, click the mouse button to establish a vertex (corner) of your polygon and drag the cross hair pointer to draw the first side of the polygon. As you draw, a single mouse click indicates the end of a line and a double mouse click closes the polygon. When you close the polygon, the cross hair pointer changes to a small square pointer. The polygon must have at least three sides.

To create a perfectly square or perfectly circular picture box

1. Select the **Rectangular Picture Box**, **Rounded-Corner Rectangular Picture Box**, or **Oval Picture Box** tool from the Tool palette.

2. Position the picture box tool on the page where you want to place the picture.

3. Hold down the **Shift** key as you click the mouse button and drag the cross hair pointer to create the box to size.

To create a text box

1. Select the **Text Box** tool and position the tool on the page where you want to place the text box.

2. Click the mouse button and drag the cross hair pointer to create the text box to size.

   If you select the Automatic Text Box check box in the New dialog box, the program automatically creates text boxes (bounded by the margin guides) on each page.

To modify a picture box or text box

1. Select the **Item** tool and activate the text box or picture box you want to modify.

2. From the Item menu, select Modify (or press ⌘-**M**).

   The program displays the Text Box Specifications or Picture Box Specifications dialog box.

3. To modify the size of the box, enter dimensions in the Width and Height fields. For more information, see *Modifying Items*.

4. To move the box, enter position coordinates in the Origin Across and Origin Down fields. For more information, see *Modifying Items*.

5. Click the OK button.

Measurements palette method

1. Activate the text box or picture box you want to modify.

2. In the Measurements palette, enter size measurements in the W and H fields and position coordinates in the X and Y fields.

Check Spelling

Purpose

Checks the spelling of words in your document by comparing them to the 80,000-word QuarkXPress dictionary and an auxiliary dictionary. Both the QuarkXPress dictionary and the auxiliary dictionary must be in the QuarkXPress folder (the folder you set up when installing the program) or in the System Folder.

To check and correct the spelling of a word

1. Highlight the word you want to check.

   or

   Position the insertion bar in the word you want to check.

2. From the Utilities menu, select Check Spelling. From the Check Spelling submenu, select Word (or press ⌘-**W**).

   If you spelled the word incorrectly, a dialog box displays alternative selections from the dictionary files or the following message:

   ```
   No similar words found
   ```

   (If you spelled the word correctly, the program highlights the word in the selections from the dictionary files.)

3. To correct the spelling of the word, click the appropriate replacement word and then click the Replace button.

   or

   Double-click the appropriate replacement word.

   or

   If no similar words are in the dictionary, click the word to display it in the correction field, and then make corrections.

To check and correct the spelling of a story

1. Select the Content tool and activate one of the text boxes in the story (the text in a set of linked text boxes) you want to check.

2. From the Utilities menu, select Check Spelling. From the Check Spelling submenu, select Story (or press ⌘-Option-W).

   A dialog box displays the total number of words in the story and the number of *Suspect words*, the words the program does not find in the dictionaries.

3. Close the dialog box by pressing Enter or by clicking the OK button.

   For each Suspect word, a dialog box displays alternative selections from the dictionary files and awaits your response.

4. To correct the spelling of a Suspect word, click the appropriate replacement word and then click the Replace button.

   or

   Double-click the appropriate replacement word.

   or

   If no similar words are in the dictionary, click the word to display it in the correction field, and then make corrections.

   or

   Select Skip (if you do not want to change the Suspect word).

To check and correct the spelling in a document or on a master page

1. Open the QuarkXPress document you want to check.

2. From the Utilities menu, select Check Spelling. From the Check Spelling submenu, select Document to check the spelling in a document or select Word (or press ⌘-W) to check the spelling on a master page.

   A dialog box displays the total number of words in the document and the number of *Suspect words*, the words the program does not find in the dictionaries.

3. Close the dialog box by pressing **Enter** or by clicking OK.

   For each Suspect word, a dialog box displays alternative selections from the dictionary files and awaits your response.

4. To correct the spelling of a Suspect word, click the replacement word and then click the Replace button.

   or

   Double-click the replacement word.

   or

   If no similar words are in the dictionary, click the word to display it in the correction field, and then make corrections.

   or

   Select Skip (if you do not want to change the Suspect word).

Colors

Purpose

Enables you to specify colors for selected items (including text, lines, backgrounds, frames, and imported black-and-white pictures) on a page, using the program's default colors or colors you create.

To define a color

1. From the Edit menu, select Colors.

   The program displays the Colors for *documentname* dialog box.

2. Click the New button.

   The program displays the Edit Color dialog box.

3. From the Model pop-up menu, select the color model (HSB, RGB, CYMK, PANTONE, TRUMATCH, or FOCOLTONE) you want to use.

4. If you select HSB or RGB, the program displays a color wheel. You can select a color from the wheel or enter numeric color component values in the Red, Green, and Blue fields.

   To define a color by selecting it from the color wheel, click the mouse button on the color you want to use. The color appears in the New part of the New/Old area of the Edit Color dialog box.

   To define a color by using numeric color component values, enter values (from 1 to 100 percent) in the Red, Green, and Blue fields of the Edit Color dialog box.

   To change the brightness of a color in the HSB or RGB models, use the vertical scroll bar to the right of the color wheel.

   If you select CMYK, enter numeric color component values (from 1 to 100 percent) in the Cyan, Magenta, Yellow, and Black fields of the Edit Color dialog box.

   If you select PANTONE, TRUMATCH, or FOCOLTONE, the program displays the PANTONE, TRUMATCH, or FOCOLTONE Color Selectors. Select a color from the Selector by entering the appropriate color number in the PANTONE No. field. (Another way to select a PANTONE color is to scroll through the list of PMS colors and click the color you want to use.)

5. If the color you are creating is a process color, click the On button in the Process Separation area of the

Edit Color dialog box; if the color you are creating is a spot color, click the Off button. (See also *Process Color* and *Spot Color*.)

6. To add the color to the color palette, enter a name for the color in the Name field, and then click the OK button in the Edit Color dialog box.

7. To save the color and include it in the document color palette, click the Save button in the Colors dialog box.

To edit a color

1. From the Edit menu, select Colors.

   The program displays the Colors for *documentname* dialog box. If you perform this step when no document is open, your changes affect the default color palette.

2. From the Color list, select the color you want to edit.

3. Click the Edit button.

   The program displays the Edit Color dialog box. The original color appears in the New and Old fields.

4. Make changes in the New field by following steps 2 through 6 for defining a color.

5. To save your changes, click the Save button.

To duplicate a color

1. From the Edit menu, select Colors.

   The program displays the Colors for *documentname* dialog box.

2. From the Color list, select the color you want to duplicate.

3. Click the Duplicate button.

   The program displays the Edit Color dialog box. The original color appears in both the New and Old fields. In the Name field, the program automatically names the duplicate color Copy of *colorname*.

4. To change the name of the duplicate color, type a new name in the Name field.

5. Make any changes to the color by following steps 2 through 6 for defining a color.

6. To save your changes, click the Save button.

To delete a color from the active document's color palette

1. From the Edit menu, select Colors.

   The program displays the Colors for *documentname* dialog box.

2. From the Color list, select the color you want to delete.

3. Click the Delete button.

4. To save the change, click the Save button.

To add a color from another QuarkXPress document to the active document's color palette

See *Append*.

To color text

1. Select the Content tool and then select the text you want to color.

2. From the Style menu, select Color. From the color selector submenu, select the color you want to use.

3. Click the OK button.

To print color separations

1. From the File menu, select Print (or press ⌘-P).

   The program displays the Print dialog box.

2. In the Color area, select the Make Separations check box.

3. From the Plate pop-up menu, select the colors of the plates you want to print. To print all colors in the document, select All Plates.

4. To print, click the OK button.

Columns

Purpose

Divides text vertically to increase readability and to add visual interest to a page.

To specify the number of columns in a new document

1. From the File menu, select New.

   The program opens a new document and displays the New dialog box.

2. In the Columns field, enter the number of columns (from 1 to 30) you want the document to have.

   This step sets the number of columns for the document's original Master Page A.

3. To specify the amount of space between columns, enter a value (from 3 to 288 points or from 0 to 4 inches) in the Gutter Width field.

To specify the number of columns in a text box

1. Select the Item tool and activate the text box for which you want to specify the number of columns.

2. From the Item menu, select Modify.

   The program displays the Text Box Specifications dialog box.

3. In the Columns field, enter the number of columns (from 1 to 30) you want the text box to have.

4. To specify the amount of space between columns, enter a value (from 3 to 288 points or from 0 to 4 inches) in the Gutter Width field.

Measurement palette method

1. Select the Item tool and activate the text box for which you want to specify the number of columns.

2. In the Cols. field of the Measurements palette, enter the number of columns (from 1 to 30) you want the text box to have.

To modify column guides on a master page

1. From the Page menu, select Master Guides.

   The program displays the Master Guides dialog box.

2. Modify the values in the Column Guides area of the Master Guides dialog box.

   The program changes the column guides on the document's Master Page A and on all pages in the document based on Master Page A.

Constraining

Purpose

Prevents you from moving or sizing items beyond the bounds of the constraining box (usually a text box).

To enable or disable automatic constraining

1. From the Edit menu, select Preferences. From the Preferences submenu, select General.

2. Select or deselect the Auto Constrain check box.

To override automatic constraining for a group

1. Select the Item tool and then select the constrained group for which you want to override the Auto Constrain setting.

2. From the Item menu, select Constrain or Unconstrain.

To make a text box or picture box a constraining box

1. Select the Item tool.

2. Hold down the Shift key as you click the items you want to constrain. The group of items must include a text box or picture box that completely contains and is behind all the other items.

3. Use the Item tool to activate the group.

4. From the Item menu, select Constrain.

Caution

If you delete a constraining box, you delete all items contained in that box.

Continued on (from)

Purpose

Creates "continued on page..." and "continued from page..." messages.

To create a "continued on page..." message

1. Use the Text Box tool to create a new text box below or at the bottom of the text box where you want the "continued on page..." message to appear. For more information, see *Boxes*.

2. Enter the text you want to use as the "continued on page..." message. At the position in the message where you want the page number to appear, press ⌘-4.

   The program inserts a page number and updates it when you modify the position of pages in the document.

To create a "continued from page..." message

1. Use the Text Box tool to create a new text box above or at the top of the text box where you want the "continued from page..." message to appear. For more information, see *Boxes*.

2. Enter the text you want to use as the "continued from page..." message. At the position in the message where you want the page number to appear, press ⌘-2.

   The program inserts a page number and updates it when you modify the position of pages in the document.

Copy

Purpose

Copies selected items to the Clipboard. You then can paste the copied items from the Clipboard to other locations.

To copy text

1. Select the text you want to copy.
2. From the Edit menu, select Copy (or press ⌘-C).
3. Position the insertion bar where you want to place a copy of the text.
4. From the Edit menu, select Paste (or press ⌘-V).

To copy a text box or picture box

1. Select the Item tool and activate the text box or picture box you want to copy.
2. From the Edit menu, select Copy (or press ⌘-C).
3. Position the insertion bar where you want to place a copy of the box.
4. From the Edit menu, select Paste (or press ⌘-V).
5. Use the Item tool to drag the copied box into place.

You cannot copy a text box that is part of a linked chain. For more information, see *Linking*.

Default Settings

Purpose

Provides a predefined value or specification for QuarkXPress features.

You can use the program's default settings or change the defaults for a specific document or for all QuarkXPress documents (applicationwide). To change preferences for a specific document, modify the preferences when

the document is open. To change preferences for all
documents, modify the preferences when no documents
are open.

To change default settings for General Preferences

1. From the Edit menu, select Preferences. From the
   Preferences submenu, select General.

   or

   Press ⌘-Y.

   The program displays the General Preferences dialog
   box.

2. Change the settings to the values you want to use as
   defaults. (For additional information, see *General
   Preferences*.)

3. To save the new default settings, click the OK
   button.

To change default settings for Typographic Preferences

1. From the Edit menu, select Preferences. From the
   Preferences submenu, select Typographic.

   The program displays the Typographic Preferences
   dialog box.

2. Change the settings to the values you want to use as
   defaults. (For additional information, see *Typographic
   Preferences*.)

3. To save the new default settings, click the OK
   button.

To change default settings for Tool Preferences

1. From the Edit menu, select Preferences. From the
   Preferences submenu, select Tools.

   or

   Double-click a tool in the Tool palette.

   The program displays the Tool Preferences dialog
   box. (If you selected Tool Preferences by double-
   clicking a tool in the Tool palette, that tool is selected
   when the dialog box opens.)

2. Change the settings to the values you want to use as defaults. (For additional information, see *Tools Preferences*.)

3. To save the new default settings, click the OK button.

To change default settings for Application Preferences

1. From the Edit menu, select Preferences. From the Preferences submenu, select Application.

   The program displays the Application Preferences dialog box.

2. Change the settings to the values you want to use as applicationwide defaults. (For additional information, see *Application Preferences*.)

3. To save the new default settings, click the OK button.

To change default settings for character attributes or paragraph formats

1. From the Edit menu, select Style Sheets.

   The program displays the Style Sheets dialog box. The Normal style sheet contains the default character attribute and paragraph format information.

2. To edit the Normal style sheet, select it from the Style Sheet scroll list and click the Edit button.

   The program displays the Edit Style Sheet dialog box.

3. Change the settings in the Edit Style Sheet dialog box to the values you want to use as defaults.

4. To exit the Edit Style Sheet dialog box, click the OK button.

5. To save the new default settings, click the Save button.

To change default settings for the color palette

1. From the Edit menu, select Colors.

   The program displays the Default Colors dialog box. The Color scroll list contains the default color list.

2. To edit a color, select it from the Color scroll list and click the Edit button.

3. Change the settings in the Default Colors dialog box to the values you want to use as defaults.

4. To save the new default settings, click the Save button.

To change default settings for automatic hyphenation and for word and character spacing

1. From the Edit menu, select H&Js.

   The program displays the H&Js dialog box. The Standard H&J option on the H&J scroll list contains the default hyphenation rules and word and character spacing values.

2. To edit the Standard H&J specification, select it from the scroll list and click the Edit button.

   The program displays the Edit Hyphenation and Justification dialog box.

3. Change the settings in the Edit Hyphenation and Justification dialog box to the values you want to use as defaults. For more information, see *Hyphenation and Justification*.

4. To exit the Edit Hyphenation and Justification dialog box, click the OK button.

5. To save the new default setting, click the Save button.

Note

See also *Application Preferences*, *Colors*, *General Preferences*, *Hyphenation and Justification*, *Tool Preferences*, and *Typographic Preferences*.

Deleting

Purpose

Removes items from the document. You can delete an item only when it is active.

Command Reference

To delete text or pictures

1. Select the Content tool and then select the text or pictures you want to delete.

2. From the Edit menu, select Cut (or press ⌘-X) or Clear (or press ⌘-K).

   or

   Press Del.

To delete a text box or picture box

1. Select the Item tool and activate the text box or picture box you want to delete.

2. From the Edit menu, select Cut (or press ⌘-X) or Clear (or press ⌘-K).

   or

   Press Del.

To delete drawn lines

1. Select the Item tool and activate the line you want to delete.

2. From the Edit menu, select Clear (or press ⌘-K).

   or

   Press Del.

To delete a group of items

From the Item menu, select Delete.

or

From the Edit menu, select Clear (or press ⌘-K).

To delete pages

1. From the Page menu, select Delete.

   The program displays the Delete dialog box.

2. In the first field, enter the page number of the first page you want to delete. To delete only one page, enter its page number in the first field.

QuarkXPress 3.1 Quick Reference

3. In the second field, enter the page number of the last page you want to delete.

4. Click the OK button.

or

1. From the View menu, select Thumbnails.

2. Drag the icon of the page you want to delete to the Trash.

or

1. From the View menu, select Show Document Layout.

   The program displays the Document Layout palette.

2. Drag the icon of the page you want to delete to the Trash.

Keyboard method

Operation	Shortcut
Delete preceding character	**Del**
Delete highlighted characters	**Del**
Delete next character	**Shift-Del**
Delete next word	**⌘-Shift-Del**
Delete a handle on a polygon box	**⌘-click** (the handle)
Delete runaround polygon	**⌘-Shift-click** (the polygon)
Delete ruler guides	**Option-click** (the ruler)

Note

Selecting Cut from the Edit menu is the only QuarkXPress delete operation that places the deleted item on the Clipboard for temporary storage (and for retrieval, if you change your mind about the deletion).

Duplicating Items

Purpose

Duplicates boxes, lines, and groups of items. To duplicate an item several times, you can use Step and Repeat, which also enables you to control the offset (the distance from the original item) of each duplicate.

To duplicate an item

1. Select the Content tool or the Item tool and then select the item you want to duplicate.

2. From the Item menu, select Duplicate (or press ⌘-**D**).

   The program duplicates the item and offsets the duplicate from the original by the values last used in the Step and Repeat dialog box.

3. If necessary, drag the duplicate to a different location.

To duplicate an item by using Step and Repeat

1. Select the Content tool or the Item tool and then select the item you want to duplicate.

2. From the Item menu, select Step and Repeat (or press ⌘-**Option-D**).

   The program displays the Step and Repeat dialog box.

3. In the Repeat Count field, enter the number of times you want to duplicate the item.

4. In the Horizontal Offset and Vertical Offset fields, enter the distance (from –24 to 24 inches) you want to offset the duplicate from the original. The default offset is .25 inch.

   A positive Horizontal Offset number places copies to the right of the original; a negative number places copies to the left of the original. A positive Vertical Offset number places copies below the original; a negative number places copies above the original.

5. Click the OK button.

Exporting Text

Purpose

Exports text from a QuarkXPress document to another application, such as a word processor.

The QuarkXPress folder must contain the import/export filter for the file format to which you want to export the text. Unless you specify that you want to export the text in ASCII format, the exported text keeps the character attributes and paragraph formats you assigned in the QuarkXPress document.

To export text

1. Select the Content tool and activate the text box that contains the text you want to export. To export only a portion of the text in the text box, select the text.

2. From the File menu, select Save Text.

    The program displays the Save Text dialog box. If you selected the entire text box, the Entire Story option button is selected. If you highlighted a portion of the text, the Selected Text option button is selected.

3. In the Save text as field, enter a name for the text file.

4. From the Format pop-up menu, select the format to which you want to export the text.

5. From the scroll list, select the location where you want to save the exported text file.

6. Click the Save button.

Find/Change

Purpose

Enables you to search for and replace text (characters, words, or sets of words) or text attributes (font, font size, or style) within a story, throughout the document, or on every master page.

To search and replace within an active text box or story (a linked chain of text boxes), activate the text box or story and position the insertion bar where you want the operation to begin. To search and replace throughout a document, open the document, but select no text boxes. To search and replace every master page in the document, open a master page, but select no text boxes.

To search for and replace text

1. From the Edit menu, select Find/Change (or press ⌘-F).

   The program displays the Find/Change dialog box.

2. In the Find what field, enter the text string for which you want to search (up to 80 characters).

3. In the Change to field, enter the text string with which you want to replace the text string in the Find what field.

   To delete the text string in the Find what field, leave the Change to field blank.

4. To search for and replace the text string throughout the document, select the Document check box.

   To search for and replace the text string in the active box or text chain only, deselect the Document check box.

5. To search for and replace the text string in the Find what field only when it occurs as an entire word, select the Whole Word check box.

   To search for and replace the text string even when it is embedded within other text, deselect the Whole Word check box.

6. To search for and replace uppercase and lowercase variations of the text string, select the Ignore Case check box.

   To search for and replace only exact matches of the text string (with respect to case), deselect the Ignore Case check box.

7. To find the first occurrence of the text string in the Find what field, hold down the Option key and click

the Find First button. (When you hold down the **Option** key, the Find Next button changes to the Find First button.)

To find the next occurrence of the text string in the Find what field, click the Find Next button.

8. To replace the highlighted occurrence of the text string with the text string in the Change to field, click the Change button.

To replace the highlighted occurrence of the text string with the text string in the Change to field and then find the next occurrence, click the Change, then Find button.

To replace the highlighted occurrence and all other occurrences of the text string with the text in the Change to field, click the Change All button.

To use a wildcard character in the Find what field

A wildcard character indicates any character. For example, entering the wildcard character **\?** in **h\?t** in the Find what field locates the words *hot*, *hat*, *hit*, and *hut*. The wildcard character does not work in the Change to field.

1. From the Edit menu, select Find/Change (or press **⌘-F**).

   The program displays the Find/Change dialog box.

2. In the Find what field, position the insertion bar where you want to enter the wildcard character.

3. Press **⌘-Shift-?** .

   The program displays \ ? in the Find what field.

To search for and replace nonprinting characters

1. From the Edit menu, select Find/Change (or press **⌘-F**).

   The program displays the Find/Change dialog box.

2. In the Find what or Change to field, position the insertion bar where you want to enter a nonprinting character.

3. Hold down the **Option** key as you press the keys for the nonprinting character.

Keys	*Effect*
\t	Searches for or replaces **Tab**.
\p	Searches for or replaces **Enter**.
\c	Searches for or replaces a New Column marker.
\b	Searches for or replaces a New Page marker.
\n	Searches for or replaces a New Line (soft return) marker.

To search for and replace text attributes

1. From the Edit menu, select Find/Change (or press ⌘-**F**).

   The program displays the Find/Change dialog box.

2. Set the search criteria in the Find what, Change to, Document, Whole Word, and Ignore Case fields. For more information, see the preceding sets of steps.

3. Deselect the Ignore Attributes check box.

   The dialog box expands.

4. In the Find what area, set the Text, Font, Size, and Style search criteria.

   To search for a text string, enter up to 80 characters of text in the Text field and select the Text check box. To search for character attributes only, deselect the Text check box.

   To search for a font, enter the name of the font in the Font field and select the Font check box. To search for text, size, or style only (regardless of the font), deselect the Font check box.

   To search for a font size, enter the size in the Size field and select the Size check box. To search for text, font, or style only (regardless of the size), deselect the Size check box.

To search for styles, select, deselect, or make gray (double-click) the check box for each style and select the Style check box.

> If you select a style's check box, the program finds the text that *does* have that style attribute.
>
> If you deselect a style's check box, the program finds the text that *does not* have that style attribute.
>
> If you make a style's check box gray, the program finds the text *regardless of* that style attribute.

To search for text, font, and size only (regardless of the style), deselect the Style check box.

5. In the Change to area, set the Text, Font, Size, and Style replacement criteria.

   To replace the text string in the Find what area, enter up to 80 characters of replacement text in the Text field and select the Text check box. To delete the text, leave the Text field empty and select the Text check box. Otherwise, deselect the Text check box.

   To replace the font in the Find what area, enter the name of the replacement font in the Font field and select the Font check box. Otherwise, deselect the Font check box.

   To replace the font size in the Find what area, enter the replacement size in the Size field and select the Size check box. Otherwise, deselect the Size check box.

   To replace the styles in the Find what area, select, deselect, or make gray (double-click) the check box for each replacement style and select the Style check box.

   > If you select a style's check box, the program *applies* that style attribute to the replacement text.
   >
   > If you deselect a style's check box, the program *deletes* that style attribute from the replacement text.

> If you make a style's check box gray, the program *keeps* that style attribute in the replacement text.

> Otherwise, deselect the Style check box.

6. To find the first occurrence of the text or attributes in the Find what field, hold down the Option key and click the Find First button. (When you hold down the Option key, the Find Next button changes to the Find First button.)

   To find the next occurrence of the text or attributes in the Find what field, click the Find Next button.

7. To replace the highlighted occurrence of the text or attributes with the text or attributes in the Change to field, click the Change button.

   To replace the highlighted occurrence of the text or attributes with the text or attributes in the Change to field and then find the next occurrence, click the Change, then Find button.

   To replace the highlighted occurrence and all other occurrences of the text or attributes with the text or attributes in the Change to field, click the Change All button.

Font Handling

Purpose

Controls the size and appearance of the type characters in a document.

To change the font

1. Select the Content tool and then select the text for which you want to change the font.

2. From the Style menu, select Font. From the Font submenu, select the font you want to use.

Measurements palette method

1. In the Measurements palette, click the font name.

2. Begin typing the name of the font you want to use. (This font must be available on your system.)

   As soon as you type enough letters for the program to recognize the font name, the complete font name appears.

3. To apply the new font, press Enter.

To change the font size

1. Select the Content tool and then select the text for which you want to change the font size.

2. From the Style menu, select Size. From the Size submenu, select the font size you want to use or select Other. (The gray font sizes are not installed in the System Folder.)

   If you select Other, the program displays the Other dialog box. In the Font Size field, enter the new size (in increments of .001 of any measurement unit). The screen display of the font may look odd (unless you use Adobe Type Manager), but the printed characters look fine.

   The program changes the font size of the selected text.

Keyboard method

To increase font size through the range of fixed size settings (from 7 to 192 points), press ⌘-Shift->.

To increase font size in 1-point increments (from 2 to 720 points), press ⌘-Option-Shift->.

To decrease font size through the range of fixed size settings (from 7 to 192 points), press ⌘-Shift-<.

To decrease font size in 1-point increments (from 2 to 720 points), press ⌘-Option-Shift-<.

Measurements palette method

1. In the Measurements palette, click the font size number.

2. Type the font size you want to use and press Enter.

   or

1. In the Measurements palette, click the font size arrow.
2. Select a font size from the Size pop-up menu.

To change the type style

1. Select the Content tool and then select the text for which you want to change the type style.
2. From the Style menu, select Type Style. From the Type Style submenu select the type style you want to use.

   The program changes the type style of the selected text.

Keyboard method

1. Select the Content tool and then select the text for which you want to change the type style.
2. Use the keyboard shortcut for the type style you want to use:

Style	*Shortcut*
Plain	⌘-Shift-P
Italic	⌘-Shift-I
Underlined	⌘-Shift-U
Word Underlined	⌘-Shift-W
Strike Thru	⌘-Shift-/
Outline text	⌘-Shift-O
Shadow text	⌘-Shift-S
All Caps	⌘-Shift-K
Small Caps	⌘-Shift-H
Superscript text	⌘-Shift-+
Subscript text	⌘-Shift-hyphen
Superior text	⌘-Shift-V

   The program changes the type style of the selected text.

To color text

1. Select the Content tool and then select the text to which you want to apply a color.

2. From the Style menu, select Color. From the Color submenu, select the color you want to apply to the text. (The Color submenu lists the colors available in the document's color palette. For more information on colors, see *Colors*).

To change the shade (intensity) of text

1. Select the Content tool and then select the text for which you want to change the shade.

2. From the Style menu, select Shade. From the Shade submenu, select a shade percentage or select Other.

   If you select Other, the program displays the Shade dialog box. Enter a shade value (from 0 to 100 percent in .1-percent increments) and click the OK button.

To change the horizontal scale of text

1. Select the Content tool and then select the text for which you want to change the horizontal scale (the horizontal compression or expansion).

2. From the Style menu, select Horizontal Scale.

   The program displays the Horizontal Scale dialog box.

3. Enter a horizontal scale value (from 25 percent to 400 percent of the default character width). The default character width is 100 percent.

To change kerning

See *Kerning*.

To change tracking

See *Tracking*.

To shift characters above or below the baseline

See *Baseline Shift*.

To make multiple changes at one time
1. Select the Content tool and then select the text you want to change.
2. From the Style menu, select Character (or press ⌘-Shift-D).

   The program displays the Character Attributes dialog box.
3. Enter values in the Font, Size, Style, Color, Shade, Horizontal Scale, Track Amount, and Baseline Shift fields according to the guidelines in the preceding sets of steps.
4. To apply the changes, click the OK button.

Font Usage

Purpose

Lists the type fonts you are using in the active document and enables you to replace a font with another font.

To change the fonts used in a document
1. Open the document.
2. From the Utilities menu, select Font Usage.

   The program displays the Font Usage dialog box. The Find what pop-up menu lists the fonts.
3. Select the font you want to change from the Find what pop-up menu.
4. Select the replacement font from the Change to pop-up menu.
5. To change the font in the Find what area to a different style (bold, italic, and so on), select, deselect, or make gray (double-click) the check box for each style in the Change to area.

   If you select a style's check box, the program *applies* that style attribute to the replacement font.

If you deselect a style's check box, the program *deletes* that style attribute from the replacement font.

If you make a style's check box gray, the program *keeps* that style attribute the same in the replacement text.

6. Begin the font replacement by clicking the Find Next button.

    The program highlights the first occurrence of the font in the Find what field.

7. To replace the font you used in the highlighted text with the font and style you selected in the Change to area, click the Change button.

    To change this occurrence of the font you used in the highlighted text with the font and style you selected in the Change to area and then find the next ocurrence, click Change, then Find button.

    To replace all occurrences of the font you used in the highlighted text with the font and style you selected in the Change to area, click the Change All button.

Note

To ensure that your document prints correctly, check the list of fonts in the Find/What pop-up menu to make sure you have the PostScript printer fonts for each screen font.

Frames

Purpose

Enables you to create borders around a text box, a picture box, or a group of boxes.

To specify whether frames appear inside or outside boxes

1. From the Edit menu, select Preferences. From the Preferences submenu, select General.

    The program displays the General Preferences dialog box.

2. In the Framing pop-up menu, select Inside or Outside.

3. Click the OK button.

To create a frame around a box

1. Activate the text box or picture box around which you want to create a frame.

2. From the Item menu, select Frame (or press ⌘-**B**).

   The program displays the Frame Specifications dialog box.

3. In the Style scroll box, select a frame style.

4. In the Width field, enter the width of the frame (from .001 to 504 points).

5. From the Color pop-up menu, select the frame color.

6. In the Shade field, enter the shade (the color saturation) of the frame (in .1-percent increments).

7. Click the OK button.

To change the distance between the frame and the text

1. From the Item menu, select Modify. From the Modify submenu, select Text Inset.

   The program displays the Text Box Specifications dialog box.

2. In the Text Inset field, enter the distance between the frame and the text (in points).

To remove a frame from a box

1. Activate the text box or picture box from which you want to remove a frame.

2. From the Item menu, select Frame (or press ⌘-**B**).

   The program displays the Frame Specifications dialog box.

3. Enter **0** in the Width field.

4. Click the OK button.

General Preferences

Purpose

Specifies how QuarkXPress displays pages on-screen. To change General Preferences for a specific document, modify the preferences when the document is open. To change preferences for all documents, modify the preferences when the document is closed.

To change a General Preferences setting

1. From the Edit menu, select Preferences. From the Preferences submenu, select General (or press ⌘-Y).

   The program displays the General Preferences dialog box.

2. From the Horizontal measure pop-up menu, select the measurement system that QuarkXPress uses for the ruler at the top of the document window:

Unit	Effect
Inches	Displays inches; divides inches into sixteenths. This option is the default measurement system.
Inches Decimal	Displays inches; divides inches into tenths.
Picas	Displays inches; divides inches into twelfths (each mark indicates .5 pica).
Points	Displays inches; divides inches into twelfths (each mark indicates 12 points).
Millimeters	Displays millimeters.
Centimeters	Displays centimeters.
Ciceros	Displays ciceros (a French measure equal to 4.552 millimeters).

Command Reference

Unit	*Effect*
Ciceros/Centimeter	Overrides the standard cicero-to-centimeter ratio; enter a new ratio in the field.

3. From the Vertical measure pop-up menu, select the measurement system that QuarkXPress uses for the ruler at the side of the document window.

4. From the Auto Page Insertion pop-up menu, select whether (and where) QuarkXPress automatically inserts pages when you import text that overflows the text box.

5. From the Framing pop-up menu, select whether QuarkXPress places frames inside or outside text boxes and picture boxes.

6. From the Guides pop-up menu, select whether QuarkXPress places ruler and page guides in front of or behind all objects on a page.

7. From the Item Coordinates pop-up menu, select whether QuarkXPress begins the scale for the horizontal ruler from zero for each page or continues the scale across the spread.

8. From the Auto Picture Import pop-up menu, select whether QuarkXPress automatically updates any pictures modified since the last time you opened the document.

9. From the Master Page Items pop-up menu, select whether QuarkXPress saves or deletes modified master page items when you apply a new master page to document pages.

10. To override the default point-to-inch ratio of 72, enter a value (from 72 to 73 in .01-point increments) in the Points/Inch field.

11. To optimize screen font resolution, smoothing the appearance of nonencrypted (Type 3) fonts on-screen, select the Render Above check box and enter a value (from 2 to 720 points in .001-point increments) in the field.

12. To change the point size below which gray bars appear instead of type, select the Greek Below check

box and enter a value in the field. The default value is 7 points.

13. To make QuarkXPress automatically create constrained relationships among newly created items, select the Auto Constrain check box.

14. Click the OK button.

Get Picture

Purpose

Enables you to import graphics into picture boxes.

You can import graphics created by painting, drawing, illustrating, or scanning programs in the following formats:

EPS (black-and-white and color)
PICT (black-and-white and color)
PNTG
TIFF and RIFF line art
TIFF and RIFF grayscale
TIFF color

To import a graphic

1. Create the picture box where you want to place the imported graphic. For more information, see *Boxes*.

2. Select the Content tool and activate the picture box.

3. From the File menu, select Get Picture (or press ⌘-E).

   The program displays the Get Picture dialog box.

4. From the Get Picture scroll box, select the file that contains the graphic you want to place in the picture box and click the Open button.

   or

   In the Get Picture scroll box, double-click the name of the file that contains the graphic you want to place in the picture box.

The program imports the graphic into the picture box.

You also can import some graphics by copying them onto the Clipboard and then pasting them into the active picture box.

To preview the graphic before importing it

Before you select the file that contains the graphic, select the Picture Preview check box in the Get Picture dialog box.

To convert an imported TIFF grayscale picture to TIFF line art

Hold down the Command (⌘) key as you click the Open button in the Get Picture dialog box.

To convert an imported TIFF color picture to TIFF grayscale

Hold down the Command (⌘) key as you click the Open button in the Get Picture dialog box.

To double the screen resolution of an imported TIFF picture

Hold down the Shift key as you click the Open button in the Get Picture dialog box.

To import the most current version of a picture file each time you open the document

1. From the Edit menu, select Preferences. From the Preferences submenu, select General.

   The program displays the General Preferences dialog box.

2. From the Auto Picture Import pop-up menu, select On.

To change the size of a picture box or its contents

See *Resizing*.

Get Text

Purpose

Enables you to import text created in other applications by using import/export filters. If you selected the corresponding filters when you installed the program, QuarkXPress text boxes accept text created in any of the following formats:

MacWrite	MacWrite II
Microsoft Word	Microsoft Works
Microsoft Write	WordPerfect
WriteNow	ASCII

To import text

1. Create the text box where you want to place the imported text. For more information, see *Boxes*.

2. Select the **Content** tool and activate the text box.

3. From the File menu, select Get Text (or press ⌘-**E**).

   The program displays the Get Text dialog box.

4. From the scroll box, select the file that contains the text you want to place in the text box.

5. To convert double hyphens in the imported text to em dashes, foot marks (') to apostrophes, and inch marks (") to quotation marks, select the Convert Quotes check box.

6. If you are importing a Microsoft Word text file and want to append the Word style sheets to the document's list of style sheets, select the Include Style Sheets check box.

   If you are importing an ASCII file that contains XPress Tags, select the Include Style Sheets check box.

7. Click the Open button.

   The program imports the text into the text box.

You also can double-click the file name to select the file that contains the text you want to place in the text box.

Command Reference

To import a Microsoft Word document with its style sheets

1. Activate the text box where you want to import the Microsoft Word document and its style sheets. To append style sheets, the Microsoft Word filter must be in the QuarkXPress folder.

2. From the File menu, select Get Text.

   The program displays the Get Text dialog box.

3. In the dialog box, select the Include Style Sheets check box.

4. Click the Open button.

   QuarkXPress imports the document and adds its style sheets to the active document's available style sheets.

To change the size of a text box
See *Resizing*.

Greeking

Purpose

Displays light gray bars rather than text or light gray boxes rather than imported pictures, making screen updating faster. Greeking affects only the display of information; it does not alter how the program prints text or imported graphics.

To specify greeking preferences

1. From the Edit menu, select Preferences. From the Preferences submenu, select General (or press ⌘-Y).

   The program displays the General Preferences dialog box.

2. In the Greek Below field, enter the point size (in .001-point increments) below which you want QuarkXPress to greek text. The default value is 7 points.

3. To turn on or off the greeking of imported pictures, select or deselect the Greek Pictures check box.

4. Click the OK button.

Groups

Purpose

Enables you to combine two or more items on a page into a single unit that behaves as one item. You can group text boxes, picture boxes, lines, or groups of items.

To group two or more items

1. Select the Item tool.

2. Hold down the Shift key and click the items you want to group.

   or

   Click and hold down the mouse button just outside the items you want to group and drag the mouse to create a marquee that includes the items.

   To deselect one of the selected items, hold down the Shift key and click the item you want to deselect.

3. From the Item menu, select Group (or press ⌘-G).

   The program groups the selected items and displays a bounding box around the elements of the group.

To modify a group

You cannot modify a group that is an element in a larger group without first ungrouping the larger group.

1. Select the group, then select Modify from the Item menu (or press ⌘-M).

   or

   Use the Item tool to double-click the group.

   The program displays a Group Specifications dialog box.

2. Make changes in the Origin Across, Origin Down, Angle, or Background Color fields. For more information, see *Modifying Items*.

   3. Click the OK button.

To ungroup items

   1. Select the Item tool and click an item within the group.

      The program displays the bounding box of the group.

   2. From the Item menu, select Ungroup (or press ⌘-U) to break the grouping.

      If the group contains other groups, the Ungroup command acts only on the outermost group.

To constrain a group

See *Constraining*.

Guides and Rulers

Purpose

Provides nonprinting lines and rulers you can use as guides in placing items on a page. Guides include margin guides, column guides, and ruler guides.

The Snap to Guides command enables you to select whether the program automatically moves page elements to the closest guide when the element is within the specified Snap Distance to the guide.

To show (or hide) guides

From the View menu, select Show (or Hide) Guides.

To show (or hide) rulers

From the View menu, select Show (or Hide) Rulers (or press ⌘-R).

To turn on or off Snap to Guides

From the View menu, select Snap to Guides.

To specify the distance at which objects snap to guides

1. From the Edit menu, select Preferences. From the Preferences submenu, select General.

   The program displays the General Preferences dialog box.

2. In the Snap Distance field, enter the distance (from 0 to 100 pixels) within which you want to move the objects to the guides or rulers.

3. Click the OK button.

To specify whether guides appear in front of or behind items

1. From the Edit menu, select Preferences. From the Preferences submenu, select General (or press ⌘-Y).

   The program displays the General Preferences dialog box.

2. In the Guides pop-up menu, select In Front or Behind.

3. Click the OK button.

To specify measurement units for the rulers

1. From the Edit menu, select Preferences. From the Preferences submenu, select General (or press ⌘-Y).

   The program displays the General Preferences dialog box.

2. From the Vertical Measure pop-up menu, select the measurement system you want to use for the left ruler. From the Horizontal pop-up menu, select the measurement system you want to use for the top ruler. Options include Inches (the default), Inches Decimal, Picas, Points, Millimeters, Centimeters, and Ciceros. For more information about these measurement systems, see *General Preferences*.

3. Click the OK button.

To change the color of guides and rulers on color monitors

1. From the Edit menu, select Preferences. From the Preferences submenu, select Application.

   The program displays the Application Preferences dialog box.

2. To change the color of the margin guides, click the Margin button.

   To change the color of the ruler guides, click the Ruler button.

   To change the color of the grids, click the Grid button.

   The program displays a color wheel and controls for selecting the color. Use the controls to select the new grid color. For more information, see *Colors*.

3. Click the OK button.

To specify column guides in a new document

1. From the File menu, select New (or press ⌘-N).

   The program displays the New dialog box.

2. Enter values in the Column Guides area and make selections in the Page Size and Margin Guides fields of the dialog box.

3. Click the OK button.

To create vertical guides

1. From the Page menu, select Master Guides.

   The program displays the Master Guides dialog box.

2. To modify the lines that indicate the columns, enter a number in the Columns field.

3. Click the OK button.

Note

See also *Colors*, *Columns*, *General Preferences*, and *Margin Guides*.

Halftone Screens

Purpose

Enables the program to reproduce a continuous-tone image, such as a photograph. QuarkXPress enables you to specify the screen the program applies to imported TIFF, RIFF, and PICT pictures. (Screens make halftone images reproducible during the printing process.)

If you plan to have a service bureau print your document, ask that service bureau what setting to use for halftone printing.

To apply a halftone screen to an imported picture

1. Activate the picture box that contains the picture to which you want to apply a halftone screen.

2. From the Style menu, select one of the following commands:

   Select Normal Screen to print using a dot pattern at a 45-degree angle. The Halftone Screen selection in the Page Setup dialog box determines the number of lines per inch of the halftone screen. (To display the Page Setup dialog box, select Page Setup from the File menu or press ⌘-**Option-P**.)

   Select 60-Line Screen/0 degree to print 60 horizontal lines per inch.

   Select 30-Line Screen/45 degree to print 30 lines per inch using lines at a 45-degree angle.

   Select 20-Line Dot Screen/45 degree to print 20 lines per inch using lines of dots at a 45-degree angle.

   Select Other Screen (you also can select this command by pressing ⌘-**Shift-S**) to print using custom screens. The program displays the Picture Screening Specifications dialog box. Specify the lines per inch (lpi), angle, and pattern of the screen).

   Experiment with different screens and line angles to see the special effects you can produce.

To view the effects of the halftone specifications

1. From the Style menu, select Other Screen.

   The program displays the Picture Screening Specifications dialog box.

2. Select the Display Halftoning check box.

3. Click the OK button.

Note

To use halftone screens, the Content tool must be selected, and the picture in the picture box must be a TIFF or RIFF line art or grayscale picture or a black-and-white bitmap.

Help

Purpose

Provides an on-line help file that contains useful tips about many QuarkXPress functions. For Help to work, the XPress Help file must be in the QuarkXPress program folder or in your computer's System Folder at the time you start QuarkXPress.

To get help

From the Apple menu, select About QuarkXPress.

or

Press ⌘-?.

or

If you have the Apple Extended Keyboard, press Help.

To get help about Print options

When you select Print from the File menu (or press ⌘-P), the program displays the Print dialog box.

To display Apple's on-line help information about printing options, click the Help button.

To use Balloon Help

If you use System 7, a Help menu is available on the menu bar (to the left of the Application menu).

1. From the Help menu, select Show Balloons.

2. Position the mouse pointer on the command, control, window, or palette for which you want help. Hold the mouse in the same position for approximately one second.

The program displays a brief description of the item and its functions (in a balloon).

Hyphenation and Justification

Purpose

Enables you to make text fit better on a page. Hyphenation divides words at syllable breaks. Justification expands or condenses the spaces between characters and words, adjusting the text on the line so that the text extends from the right margin to the left margin of the column or page.

To edit hyphenation and justification specifications

1. From the Edit menu, select H&Js.

   The program displays the H&Js for *documentname* dialog box.

2. From the H&J scroll list, select the name of the H&J specification you want to edit and click the Edit button.

   The program opens the Edit Hyphenation & Justification dialog box.

3. Select or deselect the Auto Hyphenation check box. The default setting for Auto Hyphenation is off.

   Auto Hyphenation uses both a hyphenation algorithm and the rules you specify in Edit Hyphenation & Justification dialog box.

   In the Smallest Word field, enter the minimum number of characters a word must have for the program to hyphenate the word.

   In the Minimum Before field, enter the minimum number of characters a word must have before a hyphen.

   In the Minimum After field, enter the minimum number of characters a word must have after a hyphen.

Command Reference

To enable the program to hyphenate capitalized words, select the Break Capitalized Words check box.

In the Hyphens in a Row field, enter the maximum number of consecutive lines that can end with a hyphen.

In the Hyphenation Zone field, enter the distance from the right edge of text that the program can place a hyphen. If a word falls within the hyphenation zone, the program does not hyphenate the word, but moves the word to the next line in the paragraph.

4. In the Justification Method area, set the Word Spacing, Character Spacing, and Flush Zone.

   In the Minimum, Optimum, and Maximum fields in the Word Spacing area, specify the amount of space the program can add or subtract between words to justify lines of text. Enter a percentage (from 150 to 500 percent) of the inter-word space for the font you are using.

   In the Minimum, Optimum, and Maximum fields of the Character Spacing area, specify the amount of space the program can add or subtract between characters to justify lines of text. Enter a percentage (from 150 to 500 percent) of an *en space* (the width of a zero) in the font you are using.

   In the Flush Zone field, specify how the program spaces the last line of text in a justified paragraph. If the last line in a paragraph does not extend into the flush zone, the program does not justify that line.

5. To extend a single word on a line in a justified paragraph from the left indent to the right indent, select the Single Word Justify check box.

To prevent QuarkXPress from hyphenating a word

1. Select the Content tool and position the insertion bar immediately to the left of the word you do not want the program to hyphenate.

2. Press ⌘-hyphen.

To preview how QuarkXPress hyphenates a word

1. Select the word for which you want to preview hyphenation.

2. From the Utilities menu, select Suggested Hyphenation (or press ⌘-H).

   The program displays the Suggested Hyphenation dialog box that indicates the word's hyphenation points.

3. To close the dialog box, click the OK button.

To change the way QuarkXPress hyphenates a word

1. From the Utilities menu, select Hyphenation Exceptions.

   The program displays the Hyphenation Exceptions dialog box. A scroll list alphabetically lists words for which you have changed the hyphenation and displays their current hyphenation points.

2. In the field below the scroll box, enter the word you want to add to the hyphenation exceptions list, placing hyphens at appropriate points or using no hyphens (if you do not want the program to hyphenate the word).

3. To add the word to the list, click the Add button.

4. To save the addition, click the Save button.

To delete words from the hyphenation exceptions list

1. From the Utilities menu, select Hyphenation Exceptions.

   The program displays the Hyphenation Exceptions dialog box. A scroll list alphabetically lists words for which you have changed the hyphenation and displays their current hyphenation points.

2. Highlight the word you want to delete from the hyphenation exceptions list.

3. Click the Delete button.

4. To save the deletion, click the Save button.

Note

See also *Alignment*.

Indents

Purpose

Specifies *indents*, the distance of the lines of text from the side of a text box or column.

To modify the indents of a paragraph

1. Select the Content tool and then select the paragraph for which you want to modify the indents.

2. From the Style menu, select Formats (or press ⌘-Shift-F).

   The program displays the Paragraph Formats dialog box.

3. Enter values in the Left Indent, First Line, and Right Indent fields.

Field	*Effect*
Left Indent	Specifies the distance from the left edge of a column to the left edge of the paragraph.
First Line	Specifies the distance from the left indent to the beginning of the first line of a paragraph.
Right Indent	Specifies the distance from the right edge of a column to the right edge of the paragraph.

4. Click the OK button.

To create a hanging indent

1. Select the Content tool and then select the paragraph for which you want to create a hanging indent.

2. From the Style menu, select Formats (or press ⌘-Shift-F).

   The program displays the Paragraph Formats dialog box.

3. In the Left Indent field, specify the distance from the left edge of the column to the left edge of the paragraph.

4. In the First Line field, enter a negative value.

   A negative First Line value makes the first line of the paragraph begin to the left of the position you specified in the Left Indent field.

5. Click the OK button.

Initial Caps

Purpose

Enables you to create different types of initial caps and provides an automatic drop caps feature.

To create a standard drop cap

A drop cap is a large letter that begins a paragraph and adds a graphic element to the text.

1. Select the paragraph for which you want to create the drop cap.

2. From the Style menu, Formats.

   The program displays the Paragraph Formats dialog box.

3. Select the Drop Caps check box.

   The dialog box expands to display fields for Character Count and Line Count.

4. In the Character Count field, enter the number of characters (from 1 to 8) you want to drop.

5. In the Line Count field, enter the number of lines (from 2 to 8) you want the characters to drop.

6. Click the OK button.

   The program closes the dialog box and creates the drop cap(s). To resize the drop cap(s), follow steps 7 through 9.

7. Select the drop cap(s) you want to resize.

8. From the Style menu, select Size. From the Size submenu, select the new size or select Other.

   If you select Other, the program displays the Font Size dialog box. Enter the percentage (from 0 to 400 percent in .1-percent increments) by which you want to change the size and click the OK button.

To create a standard raised cap

A raised cap is a character that sits on the same baseline as the text that follows it, but is larger in size.

1. Select the first letter of the paragraph for which you want to create the raised cap.

2. In the Font area of the Measurements palette, select a larger size from the pop-up menu or enter a larger font size in the field.

   or

   From the Style menu, select Size. From the Size submenu, select the new size or select Other.

   If you select Other, the program displays the Font Size dialog box. Enter the percentage (from 0 to 400 percent in .1-percent increments) by which you want to change the size. and click the OK button.

To create an initial cap by using an anchored box

1. Select the Item tool and then select the box you want to use for the initial cap.

2. From the Edit menu, select Cut (or press ⌘-X) or Copy (or press ⌘-C).

3. Select the Content tool and position the insertion bar at the beginning of the paragraph.

4. From the Edit menu, select Paste (or press ⌘-**V**).

   The program anchors the box at the beginning of the paragraph. To modify the anchored box, follow steps 5 through 7.

5. Activate the anchored box.

6. From the Item menu, select Modify.

   The program displays the Anchored Text Box Specifications or Anchored Picture Box Specifications dialog box.

7. To align the anchored box with the baseline of the line of text, select Baseline.

   To align the box with the top of the tallest character in the line of text, select Ascent.

Kerning

Purpose

Improves the appearance of characters by adjusting the space between two characters. QuarkXPress provides automatic kerning, which is based on the kerning table for the font, and manual kerning, which enables you to customize the space between pairs of characters.

To use automatic kerning

1. From the Edit menu, select Preferences. From the Preferences submenu, select Typographic.

   The program displays the Typographic Preferences for *documentname* dialog box.

2. To use the kerning tables included with most fonts, select the Auto Kern Above check box and enter a font size (from 2 to 720 points, in increments of .001 of any measurement system) in the Auto Kern Above field.

Enabling automatic kerning also enables any custom tracking information specified in the Tracking Edit dialog box. (To display this dialog box, select Tracking Edit from the Utilities menu.)

To use manual kerning

1. Select the Content tool and position the insertion bar between the two characters for which you want to use manual kerning.

2. From the Style menu, select Kern.

   The program displays the Kern Amount dialog box. If you have not previously applied manual kerning to that character pair, the Kern Amount dialog box displays 0 (zero). The Kern Amount dialog box does not display automatic kerning table values.

3. In the Kern Amount field, enter a value from –500 to 500. The measurement unit for manual kerning is .005, or 1/200, *em space*. (In QuarkXPress, an em space is the width of two zeros in the current font). A negative value decreases the distance between the two characters; a positive value increases the distance.

4. Click the OK button.

You also can specify kerning by selecting Character from the Style menu and then entering a value in the Kern Amount field of the Character Attributes dialog box.

Keyboard method

1. Select the Content tool and position the insertion bar between the characters for which you want to adjust kerning.

2. To increase kerning in .05-em space increments, press ⌘-Shift-}.

   To increase kerning in .005-em space increments, press ⌘-Option-Shift-}.

   To decrease kerning in .05-em space increments, press ⌘-Shift-{.

To decrease kerning in .005-em space increments, press ⌘-Option-Shift-{.

Measurements palette method

To increase or decrease kerning in .05-em space increments, click the kerning arrows in the Measurements palette.

To increase or decrease kerning in .005-em space increments, hold down the Option key as you click the kerning arrows in the Measurements palette.

To modify a font's kerning table

1. From the Utilities menu, select Kerning Table Edit.

   The program displays the Kerning Table Edit dialog box.

2. In the scroll list of available fonts, double-click the name of the font you want to edit.

   The program displays the Kerning Values dialog box.

3. In the Pair field, enter the characters for which you want to change the kerning.

   or

   From the Kerning Values scroll list, select the pair of characters for which you want to change the kerning.

   The Value field displays the current kerning value for the pair.

4. To add a kerning value for the pair, enter the new value in the Value field and click the Add button.

   To replace a kerning value for the pair, enter the new value in the Value field and click the Replace button.

   To delete the character pair from the Kerning Values list, click the Delete button.

   To replace a modified kerning table value with the font's original value, click the Reset button.

Keyboard Shortcuts

Purpose

Provides shortcuts you can use to execute QuarkXPress commands by pressing keys or key combinations rather than by using the mouse or the palettes.

Menu command shortcuts

Command	Shortcut
Apple menu	
QuarkXPress Help	⌘-? or ⌘-/
File menu	
New file	⌘-N
Open file	⌘-O
Save file	⌘-S
Save as	⌘-Option-S
Get Text or Get Picture	⌘-E
Page Setup	⌘-Option-P
Print document	⌘-P
Quit	⌘-Q
Edit menu	
Undo	⌘-Z
Cut	⌘-X
Copy	⌘-C
Paste	⌘-V
Select All	⌘-A
Find/Change	⌘-F
Open General Preferences dialog box	⌘-Y
Open Typographic Preferences dialog box	⌘-Option-Y
Style menu	
Size, Other	⌘-Shift-\

Plain text	⌘-Shift-P
Bold text	⌘-Shift-B
Italic text	⌘-Shift-I
Underline text (including spaces between words)	⌘-Shift-U
Underline words	⌘-Shift-W
Strike Thru text	⌘-Shift-/
Outline characters	⌘-Shift-O
Shadow characters	⌘-Shift-S
ALL CAPS	⌘-Shift-K
SMALL CAPS	⌘-Shift-H
Superscript	⌘-Shift-+
Subscript	⌘-Shift-hyphen
Superior characters	⌘-Shift-V
Left align	⌘-Shift-L
Center	⌘-Shift-C
Right align	⌘-Shift-R
Justify	⌘-Shift-J
Change Leading	⌘-Shift-E
Change Paragraph Format	⌘-Shift-F
Set or change Tabs	⌘-Shift-T
Make negative of picture	⌘-Shift-hyphen
Normal contrast	⌘-Shift-N
High contrast	⌘-Shift-H
Posterized contrast	⌘-Shift-P
Other contrast	⌘-Shift-C
Other screen	⌘-Shift-S
Other width	⌘-Shift-\

Item menu

Modify	⌘-M

Command Reference

Command	*Shortcut*
Frame	⌘-B
Runaround	⌘-T
Duplicate	⌘-D
Step and repeat	⌘-Option-D
Delete	⌘-K
Group items	⌘-G
Ungroup items	⌘-U
Lock in place	⌘-L

Page menu

Go to page	⌘-J

View menu

Fit in window	⌘-O
Actual size	⌘-1
Show or hide rulers	⌘-R
Show or hide invisible characters	⌘-I
Show measurements	⌘-Option-M
Show tools	⌘-Tab

Utilities menu

Check spelling of word	⌘-W
Check spelling of story	⌘-Option-W
Show suggested hyphenation	⌘-H

Dialog box command shortcuts

OK button	**Enter**
Cancel button	⌘-period
Apply button	⌘-A
Continuous Apply mode	⌘-Option-A
Yes	⌘-Y
No	⌘-N

Select next field	**Tab**
Select preceding field	**Shift-Tab**

Text command shortcuts (Content tool selected)

Move to next character	→
Move to next word	⌘-→
Move to next line	↓
Move to next paragraph	⌘-↓
Move to preceding character	←
Move to preceding word	⌘-←
Move to preceding line	↑
Move to preceding paragraph	⌘-↑
Move to beginning of line	⌘-Option-←
Move to beginning of story	⌘-Option-↑
Move to end of line	⌘-Option-→
Move to end of story	⌘-Option-↓
Select next character	**Shift-→**
Select next word	**⌘-Shift-→**
Select next line	**Shift-↓**
Select next paragraph	**⌘-Shift-↓**
Select preceding character	**Shift-←**
Select preceding word	**⌘-Shift-←**
Select preceding line	**Shift-↑**
Select preceding paragraph	**⌘-Shift-↑**
Select beginning of line	**⌘-Option-Shift-←**
Select beginning of story	**⌘-Option-Shift-↑**
Select end of line	**⌘-Option-Shift-→**
Select end of story	**⌘-Option-Shift-↓**
Delete next character	**Shift-Del**
Delete next word	**⌘-Shift-Del**

Command	*Shortcut*
Delete preceding character	**Del**
Delete preceding word	**⌘-Del**
Increase font size by one increment in preset range	**⌘-Shift->**
Increase font size in 1-point increments	**⌘-Option-Shift->**
Decrease font size by one increment in preset range	**⌘-Shift-<**
Decrease font size in 1-point increments	**⌘-Option-Shift-<**
Increase kern/track amount in .05-em increments	**⌘-Shift-}**
Increase kern/track amount in .005-em increments	**⌘-Option-Shift-}**
Decrease kern/track amount in .05-em increments	**⌘-Shift-{**
Decrease kern/track amount in .005-em increments	**⌘-Option-Shift-{**
Increase horizontal scaling in 5-percent increments	**⌘-]**
Decrease horizontal scaling in 5-percent increments	**⌘-[**
Increase leading in 1-point increments	**⌘-Shift-"**
Increase leading in .1-point increments	**⌘-Option-Shift-"**
Decrease leading in 1-point increments	**⌘-Shift-:**
Decrease leading in .1-point increments	**⌘-Option-Shift-:**
Shift selected character(s) above the baseline in 1-point increments	**⌘-Option-Shift-+**

Shift selected character(s) below the baseline in 1-point increments	⌘-Option-Shift-hyphen
Insert page number	⌘-3
Insert page number of preceding text box	⌘-2
Insert page number of next text box	⌘-4
Insert a standard hyphen	hyphen
Insert a nonbreaking standard hyphen	⌘-=
Insert a discretionary hyphen	⌘-hyphen
Insert a nonbreaking em dash	Option-=
Insert a nonbreaking en dash	Option-hyphen
Insert a standard space	space bar
Insert a nonbreaking standard space	⌘-space bar
Insert a breaking en space	Option-space bar
Insert a nonbreaking en space	⌘-Option-space bar
Align to space	⌘-\

Item command shortcuts (Item tool selected)

Move active item left in 1-point increments	←
Move active item left in .1 point increments	Option-←
Move active item right in 1-point increments	→
Move active item right in .1-point increments	Option-→
Move active item up in 1-point increments	↑

Command	*Shortcut*
Move active item up in .1-point increments	**Option-↑**
Move active item down in 1-point increments	↓
Move active item down in .1-point increments	**Option-↓**
Move item with no constraints	**⌘-drag** (press the ⌘ key and drag the item with the mouse)
Move item with horizontal and vertical constraints	**⌘-Shift-drag**
Constrain rectangular box to square, oval box to circle, and item rotation and line angle to 0, 45, or 90 degrees	**Shift-drag**
Increase line width by one increment in preset range	**⌘-Shift->**
Increase line width in 1-point increments	**⌘-Option-Shift->**
Decrease line width by one increment in preset range	**⌘-Shift-<**
Decrease line width in 1-point increments	**⌘-Option-Shift-<**

Picture command shortcuts (Content tool selected)

Move picture in active picture box left in 1-point increments	←
Move picture in active picture box left in .1-point increments	**Option-←**
Move picture in active picture box right in 1-point increments	→
Move picture in active picture box right in .1-point increments	**Option-→**

Move picture in active picture box up in 1-point increments	↑
Move picture in active picture box up in .1-point increments	**Option-↑**
Move picture in active picture box down in 1-point increments	↓
Move picture in active picture box down in .1-point increments	**Option-↓**
Center picture in picture box	**⌘-Shift-M**
Fit picture to picture box	**⌘-Shift-F**
Fit picture to picture box and maintain aspect ratio	**⌘-Option-Shift-F**
Increase scaling of picture in 5-percent increments	**⌘-Option-Shift->**
Decrease scaling of picture in 5-percent increments	**⌘-Option-Shift-<**

Tool palette command shortcuts

Display Tool palette	**⌘-Tab**
Select next tool	**⌘-Shift-Tab**
Revert to preceding values	**⌘-Z**

Measurements palette command shortcuts

Display Measurements palette	**⌘-Option-M**
Select next field	**Tab**
Select preceding field	**Shift-Tab**
Revert to preceding values	**⌘-Z**
Apply	**Enter**
Cancel	**⌘-period**

Leading

Purpose

Improves the appearance of text by adjusting the space between lines of type and enables you to create interesting effects. Normal leading is the space between one baseline and the next baseline above or below it.

To change the leading within a text box

1. Select the Content tool and activate the text box in which you want to change the leading.

2. From the Style menu, select Leading (or press ⌘-Shift-E).

   The program displays the Leading dialog box. Unless you previously modified the leading, the Leading field contains the word auto and the program sets the leading to be 120 percent of the point size of the largest font in the line.

3. In the Leading field, enter the new leading value.

   To use *absolute leading* (to make the leading the size you specify regardless of the font size), enter a value from 0 to 1080 points.

   To use *incremental leading* (to make the leading equal to the largest font size on the line, plus or minus the value you specify), enter a value from –1080 to +1080 points. (You must use the minus sign or plus sign before the value.)

4. To save the change, click the OK button.

Keyboard method

You can use the keyboard shortcuts only if you have applied absolute or incremental leading to the paragraph.

To increase leading in 1-point increments, press ⌘-Shift-".

To increase leading in .1-point increments, press ⌘-Option-Shift-".

To decrease leading in 1-point increments, press ⌘-Shift-:.

To decrease leading in .1-point increments, press
⌘-Option-Shift-:.

Measurements palette method

Enter the new leading value in the field to the left of the up and down Leading arrows.

or

To change the leading in 1-point increments (incremental leading), click the up or down Leading arrows.

To change the leading within a paragraph format

1. From the Style menu, select Formats.

    The program displays the Paragraph Formats dialog box.

2. In the Leading field, enter the new leading value.

3. To view the effect of the change, click the Apply button.

4. To save the change, click the OK button.

To change the leading mode

1. From the Edit menu, select Preferences. From the Preferences submenu, select Typographic.

    The program displays the Typographic Preferences dialog box.

2. From the Leading Mode pop-up menu, select Typesetting or Word Processing. Typesetting (the default) measures leading from baseline to baseline. Word Processing measures leading from the ascent of a line of text to the ascent of the next line of text.

3. Click the OK button.

Libraries

Purpose

Stores collections of items that you can reuse in QuarkXPress documents. The program displays an open library as a movable palette in front of open documents. You can store up to 2,000 items in each library, and you can open more than one library at a time.

To create a new library

1. From the Utilities menu, select Library.

    The program displays the Library dialog box.

2. Click the New button.

    The program displays a directory dialog box (also named Library).

3. In the New Library field, enter the name for the new library.

4. Click the Create button.

    The program displays the new library window to the right of the document window.

To open an existing library

1. From the Utilities menu, select Library.

    The program displays the Library dialog box.

2. Select the library you want to open.

3. Click the Open button.

To add items to the library by dragging

1. Select the item(s) you want to add to the library.

2. Select the Item tool (or hold down the Command (⌘) key) and drag the item(s) into the library window. When the pointer changes to the Library pointer (a pair of spectacles), release the mouse button.

To add items to the library by pasting

1. Select the item(s) you want to add to the library.

2. From the Edit menu, select Cut (or press ⌘-X) or Copy (or press ⌘-C).

    The program places the item(s) on the Clipboard.

3. Move the pointer into the library window.

4. Click the mouse button.

The program displays the Library pointer (a pair of spectacles) and arrows that indicate where the program will place the item.

5. Position the Library pointer where you want to paste the item(s) into the library.

6. From the Edit menu, select Paste (or press ⌘-V).

To save changes to a library each time you add an entry

1. From the Edit menu, select Preferences. From the Preferences submenu, select Application.

   The program displays the Application Preferences dialog box.

2. Select the Auto Library Save check box.

3. Click the OK button.

To delete an item from the library

1. Select the item you want to delete.

2. From the Edit menu, select Cut (or press ⌘-X).

   or

   Press Del.

To label an item in the library

1. Double-click the item you want to label.

   The program displays the Library Entry dialog box.

2. Select a label from the Label pop-up menu or enter a label in the Label field. You can use the same label for more than one library entry.

To place a library entry into a document page

1. Open the library you want to use.

2. Scroll through the library by using the palette's scroll bar.

3. Click the library entry you want to use.

4. Drag the library entry into the document. Release the mouse button when the library entry is in the correct location.

Lines

Purpose

Enables you to create lines and arrows and to size and place them precisely on the page. You can select from 11 preset line styles and 6 endcap styles. You can make lines as narrow as "Hairline" or as wide as 504 points.

To draw a line

1. To draw a line at any angle, select the Line tool. To draw a horizontal or vertical line, select the Orthogonal Line tool.

   When you move the mouse pointer over the active document, the pointer changes to a cross hair (+) shape.

2. Position the cross hair pointer where you want the line to begin and drag the mouse to draw the line. Release the mouse button at the end of the line.

To change the length of a line

1. Position the pointer over one of the line's handles.

   The pointer changes to the Resizing pointer.

2. Drag the handle to resize the line. When the line is the correct length, release the mouse button.

To move a line

1. Select the Item tool and position the pointer over the line.

   The pointer changes to the Mover pointer.

2. Drag the line into position. When the line is in the correct position, release the mouse button.

To rotate a line

1. Select the Rotation tool and position the pointer on the point around which you want to rotate the line.

2. Click and hold down the mouse button.

   The pointer changes to the Arrow pointer.

3. Drag the pointer in the direction you want to rotate the line. When the line is in the correct position, release the mouse button.

To delete, duplicate, or step and repeat a line

1. Select the line you want to delete, duplicate, or step and repeat.

2. From the Item menu, select Delete, Duplicate, or Step and Repeat. For more information about Step and Repeat, see *Duplicating Items*.

To cut, copy, or paste a line

1. Select the Item tool and then select the line you want to cut, copy, or paste.

2. From the Edit menu, select Cut (or press ⌘-X), Copy (or press ⌘-C), or Paste (or press ⌘-V).

To modify a line

1. Select the line you want to modify.

2. From the Item menu, select Modify (or press ⌘-M).

    The program displays the Line Specifications dialog box.

3. To change the style of the line, select one of 11 options from the Style pop-up menu.

4. To create an arrow, select an arrow head and arrow tail from the Endcaps pop-up menu.

5. To change the thickness of the line, enter the width (from 0 to 504 points in increments of .001 of any measurement unit) in the Width field or select one of the predefined widths from the Width pop-up menu.

    One of the preset line widths is Hairline. QuarkXPress prints a Hairline line as a .25-point line on a high-resolution printer and as a .5-point line on a laser printer. If you enter a value smaller than .25 points in the Width field, the program converts the line to Hairline.

6. To apply a color to the line, select a color from the Color pop-up menu. The Color pop-up menu lists all colors in the document's current color palette.

7. To change the shade (color saturation) of the line, enter a percentage (from 0 to 100 percent in .1-percent increments) in the Shade field or select one of the predefined shades from the Shade pop-up menu.

8. To prevent an active line from printing, select the Suppress Printout check box.

9. To change the way that QuarkXPress describes lines, select an option from the Mode pop-up menu:

Option	*Effect*
Endpoints	The Left Endpoint and Right Endpoint (or Top Endpoint and Bottom Endpoint, if the line is more vertical than horizontal) fields become available in the Line Specifications dialog box.
Midpoint	The Midpoint, Angle, and Length fields become available in the Line Specifications dialog box.
Left Point	The Left Endpoint, Angle, and Length fields become available in the Line Specifications dialog box.
Right Point	The Right Endpoint, Angle, and Length fields become available in the Line Specifications dialog box.

10. Click the OK button.

To modify a group of lines

1. Select the group you want to modify.

2. From the Item menu, select Modify (or press ⌘-**M**).

   The program displays the Line Specifications dialog box.

3. Modify the style, endcaps, width, color, shade, or other attributes of the group of lines. For more information, see the preceding set of steps.

   Fields for attributes that vary among the lines in the group are blank. If you enter a value in a blank field, the program applies that value to all lines in the group.

The dimensions that appear below the Mode indicator in the Line Specifications dialog box are the dimensions of the group's bounding box.

Keyboard method

To increase the line width by one increment in the preset range, press ⌘-**Shift->**.

To increase the line width in 1-point increments, press ⌘-**Option-Shift->**.

To decrease the line width by one increment in the preset range, press ⌘-**Shift-<**.

To decrease the line width in 1-point increments, press ⌘-**Option-Shift-<**.

Measurements palette method

1. From the View menu, select Show Measurements.

   The program displays the Measurements palette.

2. To change the size or position of the active line relative to the ruler origins, modify the entries in the X and Y fields (position the insertion bar in each field and enter a new value).

Option	*Effect*
Endpoints	The X1 field displays the horizontal position of the left endpoint. The X2 field displays the horizontal position of the right endpoint. The Y1 field displays the vertical position of the left endpoint. The Y2 Field displays the vertical position of the right endpoint.
Midpoint	The XC field displays the horizontal position of the line's midpoint. The YC displays the vertical position of the line's midpoint.
Left Point	The X1 field displays the horizontal position and the Y1 field displays the vertical position of the left endpoint.

Command Reference

Option	Effect
Right Point	The X2 field displays the horizontal position and the Y2 field displays the vertical position of the right endpoint.

3. To change the width of the active line, enter a value (from 0 to 504 points in .001-point increments) in the W field.

4. To change the style of an active line, select a style from the pop-up menu that is second from the right in the Measurements palette.

5. To change the endcap of the active line, select an endcap from the pop-up menu at the right end of the Measurements palette.

Linking

Purpose

Joins, or links, two text boxes so that you can flow text between them. QuarkXPress designates text contained in a chain as a *story*. You cannot link text boxes if each already contains text, but you can link a text box that contains text to an empty text box.

To link two text boxes manually

1. Select the Linking tool. If you hold down the Option key as you select the Linking tool, the tool remains selected until you select a different tool.

2. Position the tool over the first text box in the chain and click the mouse button.

   The program displays a marquee around the text box to indicate that the text box is activated for linking.

3. Position the Linking tool over the next text box in the chain and click the mouse button.

   The program displays a *linkage arrow* (a thick gray arrow) from the first box to the second.

4. To link additional boxes, repeat steps 2 and 3.

5. When you finish linking text boxes, select a different tool.

To generate new pages for overflow text

1. From the Edit menu, select Preferences. From the Preferences submenu, select General (or press ⌘-Y).

    The program displays the General Preferences dialog box.

2. From the Auto Page Insertion pop-up menu, select one of the following options:

Option	*Effect*
End of Story	Places new pages immediately after the page that contains the last text box with text overflow.
End of Section	Places new pages at the end of the section with text overflow.
End of Document	Places new pages at the end of the document.

To break the link between two text boxes

1. Select the Unlinking tool and position the pointer inside one of the text boxes in the linked chain you want to break.

    The program displays the linkage arrows for the chain.

2. To break the link between the current box and the next box in the chain, click the end of the arrow at the bottom of the box. To break the link between the current box and the preceding box, click the point of the arrow at the top of the current box.

Locked Lines and Boxes

Purpose

Locks a line or box into place.

To lock a line or box into place

From the Item menu, select Lock (or press ⌘-I).

To unlock a line or box

From the Item menu, select Unlock.

To move a locked line or box

1. Activate the line or box you want to move.

2. From the Item menu, select Modify.

   The program displays the Line Specifications or Text Box Specifications or Picture Box Specifications dialog box.

3. Reposition the line or box by using the Origin Across and Origin Down fields in the dialog box. For more information, see *Modifying Items*.

You also can unlock the item and move it with the Item tool.

Margin Guides

Purpose

Separates the body of a document from the edge of the page.

To set the margins for a new document

1. From the File menu, select New.

   The program displays the New dialog box.

2. In the Margin Guides area of the New dialog box, enter the distance from the margin guides to the edge of the page.

   If you select the Facing Pages check box (so that the document has facing pages), the dialog box includes fields for the Inside (toward the binding) and Outside margins.

3. Click the OK button.

Document Layout palette method

1. Double-click the icon of the master page.

The program displays that master page in the Document Layout palette.

2. From the Page menu, select Master Guides.

   The program displays the Master Guides dialog box.

3. In the Margin Guides field, enter the distance from the margin guides to the edge of the page.

Master Pages

Purpose

Provides a set of instructions for formatting a page. The master page does not print, but includes items that do print on document pages.

To create a master page in a new document

Whenever you create a new document in QuarkXPress, you also create its initial master pages.

Documents with facing pages have at least three master pages: a single-sided master page, a double-sided master page, and Master Page A. Documents without facing pages have at least two master pages: a single-sided master page and Master Page A.

Master Page A contains the values you establish in the New dialog box which appears when you create a new document. To specify the number of column guides on Master Page A, enter a number from 1 to 30 in the Columns field in the Column Guides area. To create an automatic text box on the Master Page A, select the Automatic Text Box check box.

The program evenly divides the automatic text box on Master Page A and on the first page of the document into the number of columns you specify.

To create a new master page in an existing document

1. From the View menu, select Show Document Layout.

   The program displays the Document Layout palette.

2. Click the single-sided or double-sided blank master page icon at the top of the palette and drag the selected master page icon onto the scroll bar.

3. When the program displays the double-arrow pointer, move the master page icon to the position where you want to place the new master page and release the mouse button.

To name a master page

Each time you create a new master page, QuarkXPress names it. The first master page is Master Page A, the second is Master Page B, and so on.

1. From the View menu, select Show Document Layout.

   The program displays the Document Layout palette.

2. Click the icon of the master page you want to name.

   The program displays the name of the master page in the field below the master page icons.

3. Type the new name (up to 63 characters in length).

To change the order of master pages

1. From the View menu, select Show Document Layout.

   The program displays the Document Layout palette.

2. Click the icon of the master page you want to move and drag the icon onto the scroll bar.

3. When the program displays the double-arrow pointer, move the master page icon to its new position and release the mouse button.

To modify a master page's margin guides or column guides

1. From the View menu, select Show Document Layout.

   The program displays the Document Layout palette.

2. Double-click the icon of the page you want to modify.

   The program displays the page.

3. From the Page menu, select Master Guides.

   The program displays the Master Guides dialog box.

4. Enter new values in the Margin Guides or Column Guides fields.

To apply a master page format to a document page

1. From the View menu, select Show Document Layout.

   The program displays the Document Layout palette.

2. Click the icon of the master page and drag the icon onto the document page icon. When the program highlights the document page icon, release the mouse button.

To delete a master page (or document page)

1. From the View menu, select Show Document Layout.

   The program displays the Document Layout palette.

2. Click the icon of the page you want to delete and drag the page icon to the Trash. When the program highlights the Trash icon, release the mouse button.

You can delete both master pages and document pages in this manner, but you cannot undo page deletions you make in the Document Layout palette.

To control how QuarkXPress handles changes to a master page

1. From the Edit menu, select Preferences. From the Preferences submenu, select General.

   The program displays the General Preferences dialog box.

2. From the Master Page Items pop-up menu, select Keep Changes or Delete Changes. Keep Changes (the default) saves modified master items whenever you apply a new master page to a document page. (The modified items are no longer master items.) Delete Changes removes modified master items whenever you apply a new master page to a document page.

   Your selection applies to subsequently created master pages only.

Measurements Palette

Purpose

Displays a movable palette where you can make changes to the document without opening menus. The selections available in the palette vary according to the active item.

To display the Measurements palette

From the View menu, select Show Measurements (or press ⌘-**Option-M**).

To reposition an item

Change the values in the X and Y fields. X is the horizontal position; Y is the vertical position.

To resize an item

Change the values in the W and H fields. W is the width; H is the height.

To rotate an item

In the Rotation field, enter the angle of rotation (from –360 to 360 degrees in .001-degree increments).

To set the number of columns in a text box

In the Cols. field, enter the number of columns (from 1 to 30).

To modify the leading in a paragraph

Enter a value (from 0 to 1080 points in .1-point increments) in the Leading field.

To change leading in 1-point increments, click the up or down Leading arrows.

To change leading in .1-point increments, hold down the **Option** key as you click the up or down Leading arrows.

To modify the tracking in a character string

1. Position the insertion bar between two characters or to the right of a character.

2. Click the left or right Tracking arrows to decrease or increase tracking.

To modify the alignment of a paragraph

Click the left, center, right, or justified alignment icon.

To change the font of a character string

Select a font from the font pop-up menu or enter the name (or the first characters of the name) of the font in the Font field.

To apply a type style to a character string

Click one or more of the type style icons.

To specify alignment of an anchored box

Click the text ascent icon to anchor the top of the box to the text ascent; click the text baseline icon to anchor the bottom of the box to the text baseline. (These icons appear at the left end of the Measurements palette when the anchored box is selected.)

To modify a line

See *Lines*.

Note

See also *Anchored Lines and Boxes*, *Boxes*, and *Lines*.

Modifying Items

Purpose

Modifies specifications for the active text box, picture box, line, or group.

To modify a text box

1. From the Item menu, select Modify (or press ⌘-**M**).

   The program displays the Text Box Specifications dialog box. The page size determines the range of values you can enter in the dialog box.

2. To reposition the text box origin relative to the zero mark on the horizontal ruler, enter a value (in increments of .001 of any measurement system) in the Origin Across field.

3. To reposition the text box origin relative to the zero mark on the vertical ruler, enter a value (in increments of .001 of any measurement system) in the Origin Down field.

4. To set the size of the text box, enter values (in increments of .001 of any measurement system) in the Width and Height fields.

5. To rotate the text box around its center, enter a value (from –360 to 360 degrees in .001-degree increments) in the Box Angle field.

6. To set the number of columns, enter a value (from 1 to 30) in the Columns field. In the Width field, enter the column width (see step 4). The minimum column width is 10 points.

7. To set the space between columns, enter a value (from 3 to 288 points in units as small as .001 of any measurement system) in the Gutter field. The standard gutter width is 0.167 inches.

8. To set the space between the text and the inside edges of the text box, enter a value in the Text Inset field. The default is 1 point.

9. To prevent the text from printing, select the Suppress Printout check box.

10. To set the distance between the first baseline and the top of the text box, enter a value (in increments of .001 of any measurement system) in the Offset field in the First Baseline area. The default value is 1 point.

In the First Baseline area, select one of the following options from the Minimum pop-up menu:

Option	*Effect*
Cap Height	Places the cap height of the largest font on the first line of text against the text inset.
Cap + Accent	Places the space used by accent marks over capital letters in the largest font on the first line of text against the text inset.

Ascent	Places the largest font on the first line of text against the text inset. This option is the default.

11. In the Vertical Alignment area, select one of the following options from the Type pop-up menu:

Option	*Effect*
Top	Aligns text from the top of the text box.
Centered	Centers text between the top and bottom of the text box.
Bottom	Aligns text from the bottom of the text box.
Justified	Evenly spaces lines of text from the top to the bottom of the text box. This option overrides the specified leading values.

12. To specify the maximum space between paragraphs when you align text vertically, enter a value in the Inter Paragraph Max field of the Vertical Alignment area.

13. In the Background area, select a background color for the text box from the Color pop-up menu, which lists all colors in an active document's palette.

    To specify the saturation of the background color, enter a percentage (from 0 to 100 percent in .1- percent increments) in the Shade field.

14. Click the OK button.

To modify a picture box

1. From the Item menu, select Modify (or press ⌘-**M**).

    The program displays the Picture Box Specifications dialog box.

2. To reposition the picture box origin relative to the zero mark on the horizontal ruler, enter a value (in increments of .001 of any measurement system) in the Origin Across field.

3. To reposition the picture box origin relative to the zero mark on the vertical ruler, enter a value (in increments of .001 of any measurement system) in the Origin Down field.

4. To set the size of the picture box, enter values (in increments of .001 of any measurement system) in the Width and Height fields.

5. To rotate the picture box around its center, enter a value (from –360 to 360 degrees in .001-degree increments) in the Box Angle field.

6. To specify the radius of the circles forming the corners of a rounded-corner square or rectangular picture box, enter a value (from 0 to 2 inches in increments of .001 of any measurement system) in the Corner Radius field.

7. To prevent the picture from printing, select the Suppress Picture Printout check box.

8. To prevent the picture in the active picture box, the box's frame, and the background color from printing, select the Suppress Printout check box.

9. To adjust the size and scale of the picture, enter values (from 10 to 1000 percent of the original size in .1-percent increments) in the Scale Across or Scale Down fields.

10. To adjust the distance between the origin (upper left corner) of the picture box and the upper left corner of the picture, enter values (in increments of .001 of any measurement system) in the Offset Across or Offset Down fields. A positive Offset Across value moves the picture to the right; a positive Offset Down value moves the picture down.

11. To rotate the picture around its center without affecting the picture box, enter a value (from –360 to 360 degrees in .001-degree increments) in the Picture Angle field.

12. To skew (slant) the picture within the picture box, enter a value (from –75 to 75 degrees in .001-degree increments) in the Picture Skew field. A positive value slants the picture to the right; a negative value slants the picture to the left.

13. In the Background area, select a background color for the picture box from the Color pop-up menu, which lists all colors in an active document's palette.

14. In the Background area, select a predefined shade from the Shade pop-up menu.

    or

    Select Other from the Shade pop-up menu and enter the percentage of shade (from 0 to 100 percent in .1 percent increments) in the Shade field.

15. Click the OK button.

To modify an anchored text box or picture box
See *Anchored Lines and Boxes*.

Moving Items

Purpose
Moves items on a single page, between pages, or between documents. QuarkXPress automatically renumbers pages, but does not automatically change links between text boxes. To adjust text box links, see *Linking*.

To move a page or a range of pages

1. From the Page menu, select Move.

   The program displays the Move Pages dialog box.

2. In the Move page(s) field, enter the page number or page range you want to move. If the document's page numbers include a prefix, you must enter the prefix in the Move Page(s) field. To move pages with absolute page numbers (numbers that represent a page's sequential position in the document), you must enter a plus sign (+) before the page number.

3. To specify the new location for the pages, click the Before Page, After Page, or To End of Document option button.

4. If you clicked the Before Page or After Page button, enter the number of pages before or after the current location that you want to move the page(s).

Document Layout palette method

1. From the View menu, select Show Document Layout.

   The program displays the Document Layout palette (the thumbnail view of the document).

2. Click the icon of the page you want to move and drag the icon to the new location.

   To move several consecutive pages at one time, click the icon of the first page you want to move, hold down the Shift key as you click the icon of the last page in the range, and then drag the selected icons to the new location. Release the mouse button.

To move a text box or picture box by using numeric values

1. Select the Item tool and activate the text box or picture box you want to move.

2. From the Item menu, select Modify.

   The program displays the Text Box Specifications or Picture Box Specifications dialog box.

3. Enter values (in increments of .001 of any measurement system) in the Origin Across and Origin Down fields to specify the new position relative to the upper left corner of the box.

4. Click the OK button.

To move a picture box in 1-point increments

Moving a picture box in 1-point increments is called *nudging*.

1. Select the Item tool and activate the text box or picture box you want to move.

2. Press the arrow keys to nudge the picture box up, down, right, or left.

Tool palette method

1. Select the Item tool and activate the text box or picture box you want to move.

2. Drag the box to its new position.

Opening and Closing Documents

Purpose

Enables you to open up to seven documents at one time, each in a document window. (Your computer's available memory may limit the number and size of document windows.) The Close command closes the active document.

To open a new document

1. If you are not already working in QuarkXPress, open the QuarkXPress application.

2. From the File menu, select New.

   The program displays the New dialog box.

3. Enter values for Page Size, Column Guides, and Margin Guides in the dialog box fields. For more information, see *Column Guides*, *Margin Guides*, and *Page Size*.

4. Click the OK button.

   The program displays the first, blank page of the new document. Page guide lines (blue on color monitors, dotted lines on black-and-white monitors) indicate the page's margins. Page guide lines do not print.

To open an existing document

1. If you are not already working in QuarkXPress, open the QuarkXPress application.

2. From the File menu, select Open (or press ⌘-**O**).

   The program displays the Open dialog box.

3. To select whether the scroll box displays All Types (the default), Documents, or Templates, click that button at the bottom of the Open dialog box.

4. To display a thumbnail view of the first page of a template, select the Template Preview check box in the top right corner of the dialog box. (Template Preview displays thumbnail views of templates created with QuarkXPress version 2.0 or later only.)

5. In the scroll box, select the document or template you want to open and click the Open button.

or

Double-click the name of the document or template.

To access documents or templates on another drive, click the Drive button. (If you use System 7, click the Desktop button to access documents or templates anywhere on the Desktop.)

To close a document

From the File menu, select Close.

or

Click the close box in the upper left corner of the document window.

If you are closing a document you have never saved, a dialog box asks whether you want to save the document. To save the document, click the Yes button, enter a name for the document in the Save current document as field, and use the controls in the dialog box to indicate where you want to save the document.

If you are closing a document you have saved previously, a dialog box asks whether you want to save the changes to the document. To replace the preceding version of the document with the new version, click the Yes button. To abandon the changes you have made to the document since the last time you saved, click the No button. To close the Close dialog box and return to the active document, click the Cancel button.

Note

See also *Document Windows* in the QuarkXPress Basics section.

Page Numbering

Purpose

Sets up automatic page numbering in a QuarkXPress document.

To use automatic page numbering

1. From the Page menu, select Display. From the Display submenu, select the master page on which you want to begin numbering pages.

   The program displays the master page.

2. Create a text box where you want the page number to appear.

3. Select the Content tool and activate the text box where you want the page number to appear.

4. Press ⌘-3.

   The program enters the Current Box Page Number indicator in the text box. This indicator does not display the page number on-screen, but does print the page number. If you place the Current Box Page Number indicator on a master page, any pages you format according to that master page automatically include the page number.

5. Select the Current Box Page Number placeholder, ⟨#⟩, and specify its font, size, style, and so on. For more information, see *Font Handling*.

To use automatic page numbering with a section prefix

1. Open the document and display the page where you want to begin numbering the section.

2. From the Page menu, select Section.

   The program displays the Section dialog box.

3. To make the current page of the document the first page of the section, select the Section Start check box.

4. In the Prefix field, enter up to four characters for the first part of the section's page numbers. For example, to begin the section with page 5-1, enter 5- in the Prefix field.

5. In the Number field, enter the page number of the first page in the section. The default page number is 1.

6. From the Format pop-up menu, select one of the following options:

Option	Effect
1,2,3,4	Uses Arabic numerals.
I, II, III, IV	Uses uppercase Roman numerals.
i, ii, iii, iv	Uses lowercase Roman numerals.
A, B, C, D	Uses uppercase letters as numerals.
a, b, c, d	Uses lowercase letters as numerals.

The program applies the format you select to all automatic page numbers in the section.

To create jump lines

See *Continued on (from)*.

Page Setup

Purpose

Specifies the size and orientation of a page. The options in the Page Setup dialog box depend on the type of printer selected in the Chooser.

To set up pages for printing on a PostScript printer with the LaserWriter printer driver

1. Open the document you want to print.

2. From the File menu, select Page Setup (or press ⌘-Option-P).

   The program displays the Page Setup dialog box.

3. In the Paper area, select the size of paper you will use to print the document. Depending on the option you select from the Printer Type pop-up menu and the printer driver in your System Folder, you can select from up to seven standard paper sizes.

4. To scale the printing image, enter a percentage (from 25 to 400 percent of the original size) in the Reduce or Enlarge field.

5. Click one of the Orientation icons (portrait or landscape) to specify the orientation of the printed page.

6. In the Printer Effects area, select any of the following check boxes:

   Option   *Effect*

   Font   Substitutes the Times font for New
   Substitution   York, Helvetica for Geneva, and
                      Courier for Monaco. This option
                      may change the spacing of the
                      document.

   Text   Uses the program's bitmap-
   Smoothing   smoothing algorithm, improving
                      the appearance of printed text.

   Graphics   Uses the program's bitmap-
   Smoothing   smoothing algorithm, improving
                      the appearance of printed 1-bit
                      graphics.

   Faster Bitmap   Speeds up printing of the document.
   Printing

7. To open a dialog box that lists additional printing options available with your printer driver (included with your Macintosh's System software), click the Options button.

8. To display Apple's on-line help information about Page Setup, click the Help button.

9. In the Halftone Screen field, enter the number of lines per inch (from 15 to 400) you want to use for printing halftone graphics and shaded items. The default setting for a LaserWriter is 60.

10. In the Printer Type pop-up menu, select the printer you will use to print the document.

11. From the Paper Size pop-up menu, select the size of paper you will use to print the document. This pop-up menu is available only when the printer you select from the Printer Type pop-up menu can print on more than one page size.

12. In the Paper Type area, select the Paper button (if you will print the document on paper) or Film button (if you will print the document on clear film). This selection is available only when the printer you

selected from the Printer Type pop-up menu can print on film.

13. In the Resolution field, enter the resolution (from 72 to 5,000 dpi) of the printer you selected in the Printer Type field.

14. In the Paper Width field, enter the width of the paper or film. Do not exceed the printer's maximum paper width. This selection is available only when the printer you selected from the Printer Type pop-up menu is a roll-fed device.

15. In the Paper Offset field, enter the distance you want to offset the printing area from the left edge of the paper. This selection is available only when the printer you selected from the Printer Type pop-up menu is a roll-fed device.

16. In the Page Gap field, enter the vertical distance between document pages. This selection is available only when the printer you selected from the Printer Type pop-up menu is a roll-fed device.

17. Click the OK button.

To set up pages for printing on an ImageWriter printer

1. From the File menu, select Page Setup (or press **⌘-Option-P**).

   The program displays the Page Setup dialog box.

2. In the Paper area, select the size of paper you will use to print the document.

3. Click one of the Orientation icons (portrait or landscape) to specify the orientation of the printed page.

4. To eliminate the empty area at the tops and bottoms of printed pages, select the No Gaps Between Pages check box in the Special Effects area.

   The Tall Adjusted and 50 percent Reduction fields are not available when printing a QuarkXPress document.

5. Click the OK button.

Page Size

Purpose

Enables you to select one of five predefined page sizes or to specify a custom page size.

To set the page size of a new document

1. From the File menu, select New.

    The program displays the New dialog box.

2. In the Page Size area, click one of the following page size buttons:

Button	Page Size
US Letter	8.5 inches by 11 inches (the default size).
US Legal	8.5 inches by 14 inches.
A4 Letter	8.27 inches by 11.69 inches.
B4 Letter	6.93 inches by 9.84 inches.
Tabloid	11 inches by 17 inches.
Other	Enables you to specify a custom size.

3. If you clicked the Other button, enter the width and height of the document in the Width and Height fields. QuarkXPress pages can be as small as 1 inch by 1 inch or as large as 48 inches by 48 inches, but you must consider the limitations of your output device (such as your laser printer) when you specify the page size. For information on printing pages that are larger than the capacity of your printer, see *Tiling*.

4. Click the OK button.

To change the page size of an existing document

1. Open the document for which you want to change the page size.

2. From the File menu, select Document Setup.

    The program displays the Document Setup dialog box.

3. In the Page Size area, click the US Letter, US Legal, A4 Letter, B4 Letter, Tabloid, or Other page size button.

4. If you clicked the Other button, enter the width and height of the document in the Width and Height fields.

   QuarkXPress pages can be as small as 1 inch by 1 inch or as large as 48 inches by 48 inches, but you must consider the limitations of your output device (such as your laser printer) when you specify the page size. For information on printing pages that are larger than the capacity of your printer, see *Tiling*.

5. To change a single-sided document to a document with facing pages, select the Facing Pages check box.

6. Click the OK button.

Paragraph Formats

Purpose

Enables you to apply style specifications to selected paragraphs.

To apply style attributes to selected paragraphs

1. From the Style menu, select Formats.

   The program displays the Paragraph Formats dialog box.

2. To change the indents of the selected paragraphs, enter values in the Left Indent, First Line, and Right Indent fields. For more information, see *Indents*.

3. To change the leading (the space between the lines of text) in the selected paragraphs, enter a different value in the Leading field. For more information, see *Leading*.

4. To change the amount of space between the selected paragraphs, enter values (in increments of .1 of any measurement system) in the Space Before and Space After fields.

5. To lock the text in the selected paragraphs to the document's baseline grid, select the Lock to Baseline Grid check box.

6. To create initial caps in the selected paragraphs, select the Drop Cap check box.

   The program extends the dialog box. In the Character Count field, enter the number of initial cap characters (from 1 to 8). In the Line Count field, enter the number of lines (from 2 to 8) you want the initial cap characters to extend below the baseline. For more information, see *Initial Caps*.

7. To keep the last line of a paragraph with the first line of the following paragraph (if the paragraph break falls at the bottom of a column of text), select the Keep With Next ¶ check box.

8. To specify how the program breaks a paragraph that falls at the bottom of a column of text, select the Keep Lines Together check box.

   The program extends the dialog box. To specify that the program does not break a paragraph that falls at the bottom of a column of text, click the All Lines in ¶ button. To specify how the program breaks a paragraph that falls at the bottom of a column of text, enter values in the Start and End fields. The default settings of 2 and 2 indicate that the paragraph must have at least two lines at the top and the bottom of the column.

9. To change the alignment of the selected paragraphs, select Left, Right, Centered, or Justified from the Alignment pop-up menu. For more information, see *Hyphenation and Justification*.

10. To apply a different hyphenation and justification specification to the selected paragraphs, select a specification from the H&J pop-up menu. (The pop-up menu lists all H&J specifications available for the active document.) For more information, see *Hyphenation and Justification*.

11. To preview the effects of the settings in the Paragraph Formats dialog box, click the Apply button.

12. To save the changes, click the OK button.

To copy a paragraph format from one paragraph to another

1. Select the paragraph to which you want to copy the format of another paragraph.

2. Hold down the **Shift** and **Option** keys as you click the paragraph that has the format you want to copy.

    The program applies the format of the paragraph you clicked to the paragraph you selected.

PICT Files

Purpose

Stores pictures created in MacDraw, MacDraft, Cricket Draw, Cricket Graph, SuperPaint, FreeHand, Canvas, Mac3D, MiniCAD, and Pro3D.

To import a PICT file

1. Create the picture box where you want to place the imported graphic. For more information, see *Boxes*.

2. Select the **Content** tool and activate the picture box.

3. From the File menu, select Get Picture.

    The program displays the Get Picture dialog box.

4. From the scroll list, select the PICT file you want to import and click the Open button.

    or

    Double-click the file name.

Note

See also *Get Picture*.

Picture Color

Purpose

Enables you to apply color to the black value of imported black-and-white bitmap pictures and to TIFF and RIFF line art and grayscale pictures. You also can apply color to the background of pictures and to picture box frames.

To apply color

1. Select the **Content** tool.

2. From the Style menu, select Color. From the Color submenu, select a color from the document's color palette.

3. To shade the color, select Shade from the Style menu. From the Shade submenu, select a predefined shade or select Other.

    If you select Other, the program displays a dialog box. Enter the percentage of shade (from 0 to 100 percent in .1 percent increments).

To apply color to the background

1. From the Item menu, select Modify.

    The program displays the Picture Box Specifications dialog box.

2. In the Background area, select a color from the Color pop-up menu.

3. In the Background area, select a predefined shade from the Shade pop-up menu.

    or

    Select Other from the Shade pop-up menu and then enter the percentage of shade (from 0 to 100 percent in .1 percent increments) in the Shade field.

4. Click the OK button.

Picture Contrast

Purpose

Enables you to modify the contrast of imported black-and-white TIFF and RIFF pictures and color TIFF and bit-map pictures.

Contrast is the relationship between the tones (light, medium, and dark areas) of a picture. To control picture contrast in QuarkXPress, you modify a curve on a graph to control the ratio of Input (the original contrast of the picture) to Output (the modified contrast of the picture). When the curve on the graph is a 45-degree line extending from 0 to 1, the picture has normal contrast.

To change the contrast of a grayscale or black-and-white picture

1. Select the Content tool and activate the picture box that contains the picture you want to modify.

2. From the Style menu, select Other Contrast.

   The program displays the Picture Contrast Specifications dialog box.

3. Use the tools on the left side of the dialog box to modify the contrast curve in the Input-Output graph.

   When the curve on the graph is a 45-degree line extending from 0 to 1, the picture has normal contrast.

4. To reverse the contrast, select the Negative check box.

5. To preview the effect of your changes, click the Apply button.

6. To save your changes and close the dialog box, click the OK button.

To change the contrast of a color picture

1. Select the Content tool and activate the picture box that contains the picture you want to modify.

2. From the Style menu, select Other Contrast.

   The program displays the Picture Contrast Specifications dialog box.

3. In the Model area, select the color model you want to use. For more information, see *Colors*, *Spot Color*, and *Process Color*. For a detailed discussion of color models, refer to the Color chapter of the Using QuarkXPress manual.

4. In the Color area, select the first color component you want to modify. The components available in the Color area depend on the color model you selected in step 3.

5. Use the tools on the left side of the dialog box to drag the appropriate curve in the Input-Output graph, modifying the color component. (Each color component has its own curve.)

6. Repeat steps 4 and 5 to modify the other color components.

7. To preview the effect of your changes, click the Apply button.

8. To save your changes and close the dialog box, click the OK button.

To make a picture high contrast

1. Select the Content tool and activate the picture box that contains the picture you want to modify.

2. From the Style menu, select High Contrast (or press ⌘-Shift-H).

   A grayscale picture changes to a picture with two levels of gray. A color picture changes to a picture with no intermediate color saturation values.

To posterize a picture

1. Select the Content tool and activate the picture box that contains the picture you want to modify.

2. From the Style menu, select Posterized (or press ⌘-Shift-P).

   A grayscale picture changes to a picture with six levels of gray. A color picture changes to a picture with six color saturation values.

To return a picture's contrast to normal

1. Select the Content tool and activate the picture box that contains the picture you want to modify.

2. From the Style menu, select Normal Contrast (or press ⌘-Shift-N).

A grayscale picture changes to a picture with six levels of gray. A color picture changes to a picture with six color saturation values. The picture reverts to its imported contrast levels, reversing any modifications you made by using the other contrast commands.

Printing

Purpose

Prints the active QuarkXPress document.

To prepare for printing

1. To check the output device, select Chooser from the Apple menu.

2. To check the correct paper size and printing effects, select Page Setup from the File menu.

To print a document

1. From the File menu, select Print (or press ⌘-**P**).

   The program displays the Print dialog box.

2. In the Copies field, enter the number of copies you want to print.

3. To print the entire document, click the All button in the Pages area.

   To print a range of pages, enter beginning and ending page numbers in the From and To fields in the Pages area.

   To print the document for the first time or to change any fields in the Print dialog box, follow steps 4 through 13; otherwise, click the OK button to begin printing.

4. To print a cover page (a page that lists the name of the document and the time you printed it), click the First Page or Last Page button. The First Page button makes the cover page print before the document; the Last Page button makes the cover page print after the document.

5. If the printer has a paper tray that feeds sheets of paper into the printer, click the Paper Cassette button.

   If you feed sheets of paper into the printer as the document prints, click the Manual Feed button.

6. To print in color or gray tones, click the Color/Grayscale button.

7. In the Output area, click the Normal, Rough, or Thumbnails button.

Button	*Effect*
Normal	Prints the document with all text and pictures.
Rough	Prints the document with pictures displayed as boxes with simplified box frames.
Thumbnails	Prints miniature pages.

8. In the Output area, click the All Pages, Odd Pages, or Even Pages button.

9. To reverse the printing order of the pages, select the Back to Front check box.

10. To print two or more collated copies of the document, select the Collate check box.

11. To print pages in a spread contiguously, select the Spreads check box.

12. To print registration marks and crop marks outside the document page area, select the Registration Marks check box and then select whether the registration marks are Centered or Off Center relative to the crop marks.

13. To print oversized documents in pieces, or *tiles*, click the Manual or Auto Overlap Tiling button. If you click the Auto button, enter an overlap measurement in the Auto Overlap field.

14. To print a separate sheet for each color plate, select the Make Separations check box.

    The program displays the Plate pop-up menu, which lists the document's available colors. From the Plate pop-up menu, select the color of each plate you want to print. To print all colors in the document, select All Plates.

15. To print colors as shades of gray, select the Print Colors as Grays check box.

16. To print blank pages in the document, select the Blank Pages check box.

17. Click the OK button.

To monitor the progress of a print job on a PostScript printer

To display information about the page, separation plate, tile, and picture being processed, hold down the Shift key as you click the OK button in the Print dialog box.

Process Color

Purpose

Converts continuous tone color (such as the color in photographs or pictures with many colors) to line tone, which a printing press can reproduce. When you use process color, the program prints four separate plates, breaking the colors on the page into cyan, magenta, yellow, and black components.

To specify a new color as process color

1. From the Edit menu, select Colors.

   The program displays the Colors dialog box.

2. Click the New button.

   The program displays the Edit Color dialog box.

3. To make the new color a process color, click the On button in the Process Separation area.

4. Click the OK button in the Edit Color dialog box.

5. To save the changes, click the Save button in the Colors dialog box.

To change a spot color to a process color

1. From the Edit menu, select Colors.

   The program displays the Colors dialog box.

2. Click the Edit button.

   The program displays the Edit Color dialog box.

3. To change the color from a spot color to a process color, click the On button in the Process Separation area.

4. Click the OK button in the Edit Color dialog box.

5. To save the changes, click the Save button in the Colors dialog box.

To print color separations for a document with process color

1. From the File menu, select Print (or press ⌘-P).

   The program displays the Print dialog box.

2. In the Color area, select the Make Separations check box.

3. From the Plate pop-up menu, select the colors of the plates you want to print.

   To print all colors in the document, select All Plates.

4. To print, click the OK button.

Note

See also *Colors* and *Spot Color*.

Registration Marks

Purpose

Indicates the four outside corners of the document. Printers use registration marks, or *crop marks*, to determine where to trim the pages.

To use registration marks

1. From the File menu, select Print.

   The program displays the Print Dialog box.

2. Select the Registration Marks check box.

3. Click the OK button to print the document.

   or

   Close the dialog box and save the settings with the document.

Resizing

Purpose

Changes the size of items on the page.

To change the size of text characters

Select the Content tool and then select the characters you want to resize. From the size submenu, select a font size. To use a size that is not on the submenu, select Other.

If you select Other, the program displays the Font Size dialog box. Enter a font size (from 2 to 720 points in .001-point increments).

To change the size of text boxes or picture boxes

1. Select the Item tool or the Content tool and activate the box you want to resize.

2. From the Item menu, select Modify.

   The program displays the Text Box Specifications or Picture Box Specifications dialog box.

3. Enter new size values in the Width and Height fields. For more information, see *Boxes*.

4. Click the OK button.

Measurements palette method

1. Select the Item tool or the Content tool and activate the box you want to resize.

2. From the View menu, select Show Measurements.

   The program displays the Measurements palette.

3. Enter new dimensions in the W (width) and H (height) fields.

Tool palette method

1. Select the Item tool or the Content tool and activate the box you want to resize.

2. Drag one of the box handles to change the size of the box.

Rotating

Purpose

Enables you to rotate text, pictures, lines, or groups. You cannot rotate anchored boxes or lines with endpoints (such as arrows).

To rotate a text box, picture box, or group

1. From the Item menu, select Modify.

   The program displays the Text Box Specifications, Picture Box Specifications, or Group Specifications dialog box.

2. In the Angle (or Box Angle) field, enter the number of degrees (from –360 to 360) you want to rotate the text box.

3. Click the OK button.

Measurements palette method

1. From the View menu, select Show Measurements.

   The program displays the Measurements palette.

2. In the Angle field, enter the number of degrees (from –360 to 360) you want to rotate the item.

Tool palette method

1. Select the Rotation tool.

   The program displays the item's center of rotation as a circle with vertical and horizontal lines through it.

2. Drag the center of rotation to the appropriate position and click the mouse button.

3. To rotate the item, hold down the mouse button and drag the mouse in the appropriate direction.

Command Reference

The program displays a line from the mouse pointer to the center of rotation. The line indicates the angle of rotation.

Runaround

Purpose

Wraps, or *flows*, text around other items, including pictures and other text boxes, on the page. Runaround does not work with grouped items.

To control how text runs around an item

1. Activate the item around which you want to wrap the text.

2. From the Item menu, select Runaround.

    The program displays the Runaround Specifications dialog box.

3. From the Mode pop-up menu, select None, Item, Auto Image, or Manual Image.

    If you select None, text flows behind the active item. The dialog box does not provide additional options.

    If you select Item, text flows around the item. You can specify the space between the item and the text that flows around the item by entering values (in .001 increments of any measurement system) in the Top, Left, Bottom, and Right fields.

    If you select Auto Image (for picture boxes only), text flows around the active picture box, and you can specify the distance between the picture box and the text by entering a value in the Text Outset field.

    If you select Manual Image (for picture boxes only), the program creates around the picture box a runaround polygon with handles you can use to modify the way text runs around the picture box.

    > To move a handle of the runaround polygon, click and drag that handle. To constrain the movement of the handle to a horizontal or

vertical direction, hold down the Shift key as you click and drag the handle. To add a handle, hold down the Command (⌘) key and click the point in the line where you want to add the handle. To delete a handle, hold down the Command (⌘) key and click the handle you want to delete.

To move a line of the runaround polygon, click and drag that line. To constrain the movement of the line to a horizontal or vertical direction, hold down the Shift key as you click and drag the line.

If you select Manual Image, the dialog box also enables you to specify the distance between the picture and the text by entering a value in the Text Outset field and to flow the text within the runaround polygon by selecting the Invert check box.

Service Bureaus

Purpose

Prints a desktop publisher's documents on *imagesetting* devices.

To prepare a QuarkXPress file for a service bureau

Before creating the document, speak with the people at the service bureau to ensure that you set up your files and system according to their requirements.

1. Create a folder on the disk you will send to the service bureau. (Even if you send the file via modem, having everything in one folder is a good idea.)

2. Copy the QuarkXPress file into this folder.

3. Copy the XPress Preferences file (from your Macintosh's QuarkXPress folder) into this folder.

4. Copy all the picture files used in the document into this folder.

5. Send the folder to the service bureau.

Skewing

Purpose

Slants, or *skews*, a picture at an angle.

To skew a picture

1. Activate the picture box that contains the picture you want to skew.

2. From the Item menu, select Modify (or press ⌘-M).

   The program displays the Picture Box Specifications dialog box.

3. In the Picture Skew field, enter the number of degrees (from –75 to 75 in .001 degree-increments) you want to skew the picture within its box. A negative value skews the picture to the left; a positive value skews the picture to the right.

4. Make any other changes in the Picture Box Specifications dialog box. For more information, see *Boxes*.

5. Click the OK button.

Space/Align

Purpose

Aligns selected items horizontally or vertically (by their top, bottom, left, or right edges or their centers) and distributes them evenly across a specified area. Space/Align works only when two or more items are active.

To align and distribute items on a page

1. Select the items you want to align.

2. From the Item menu, select Space/Align.

   The program displays the Space/Align Items dialog box.

3. To align items horizontally, select the Horizontal check box.

4. To align items vertically, select the Vertical check box.
5. In the Space field(s), enter a percentage (from 0 to 1000 percent in .1-percent increments) or a measurement value by which you want to increase or decrease the horizontal and vertical space between the selected items.
6. To space the items evenly from left to right (for Horizontal) or top to bottom (for Vertical) click the Distribute Evenly button(s).
7. From the Between pop-up menu(s), select one of the following options:

Option	*Effect*
Items	Distributes space between items.
Left Edges or Top Edges	Distributes space between the left or top edges of items.
Right Edges or Bottom Edges	Distributes space between the right or bottom edges of items.
Centers	Distributes space between the horizontal or vertical centers of items.

8. To preview the effect of the Space/Align dialog box selections, click the Apply button.
9. To save the dialog box selections and close the dialog box, click the OK button.

Special Characters

Purpose

Produces various characters in addition to the standard text characters.

To show special characters

From the View menu, select Show Invisibles.

Special characters

Character	Shortcut
Bullet	Option-8
Cents	Option-4
Closing double quotation mark	Option-Shift-[
Closing single quotation mark	Option-Shift-]
Copyright	Option-G
Degree	Option-Shift-8
Discretionary hyphen	⌘-hyphen
Em dash	Option-Shift-hyphen
En dash	Option-hyphen
En space	Option-spacebar
Fraction bar	Option-Shift-1
Indent Here	⌘-\
New Box	Shift-Enter
New Column	Enter
New Line (not the beginning of a new paragraph)	Shift-Enter
New Paragraph	Enter
Nonbreaking en space	⌘-Option-Shift-spacebar
Nonbreaking hyphen	⌘-=
Opening double quotation mark	Option-[
Opening single quotation mark	Option-]
Page number, current	⌘-3

Page number, next text box	⌘-4
Page number, preceding text box	⌘-2
Registered trademark	**Option-R**
Tab	**Tab**
Trademark	**Option-2**
Vertical bar	**Shift-**

Spot Color

Purpose

Prints one page for each color on each page of a document.

To specify a new color as a spot color

1. From the Edit menu, select Colors.

   The program displays the Colors for *documentname* dialog box.

2. Click the New button.

   The program displays the Edit Color dialog box.

3. To make the new color a spot color, click the Off button in the Process Separation field.

4. Click the OK button in the Edit Color dialog box.

5. To save the changes, click the Save button in the Colors dialog box.

To change a process color to a spot color

1. From the Edit menu, select Colors.

   The program displays the Colors dialog box.

2. Click the Edit button.

   The program displays the Edit Color dialog box.

3. To change the color from a process color to a spot color, click the Off button in the Process Separation field.

4. Click the OK button in the Edit Color dialog box.

5. To save the changes, click the Save button in the Colors dialog box.

To print an active document that includes spot color

1. From the File menu, select Print (or press ⌘-P).

    The program displays the Print dialog box.

2. In the Color area, select the Make Separations check box.

3. From the Plate pop-up menu, select the colors of the plates you want to print. (This pop-up menu lists all the document's available colors.)

    To print plates for all colors in the document, select All Plates.

4. Click the OK button to begin printing.

Notes

When you print a document that has more than one color, the separate plates are sometimes *out of register* (not aligned correctly). This problem can cause a thin white line between two items on the page that are different colors. To avoid this problem, see *Trapping*.

See also *Colors* and *Process Color*.

Spreads

Purpose

Enables you to create layouts that span two or more side-by-side pages, or *spreads*.

To create a multipage spread in a new document

1. From the File menu, select New.

    The program displays the New dialog box.

2. Select the Facing Pages check box.
3. Click the OK button.

To create a multipage spread in a document without facing pages

1. From the View menu, select Show Document.

   The program displays the Document Layout palette.

2. Drag a master page icon from the top of the palette to the area that displays the document pages.

3. Drag each additional master page icon to the document page area, arranging the pages in the layout you want to use. You can arrange the pages in horizontal rows (up to 48 inches in total width), vertical rows, or a combination of horizontal and vertical rows.

   If a left-, right-, or down-arrow pointer appears as you drag a master page icon into position, the program repositions existing pages in the direction indicated by the arrow.

4. When you complete the arrangement of the spread, close the Document Layout palette by clicking the close box in the upper left corner of the palette.

To create a multipage spread in a document with facing pages

When you insert, delete, or move pages in a document with facing pages, QuarkXPress automatically repositions and reformats pages as needed.

1. From the View menu, select Show Document.

   The program displays the Document Layout palette.

2. Drag a master page icon from the top of the palette to the area that displays the document pages.

3. Drag each additional master page icon to the document page area, arranging the pages in the layout you want to use.

   The program displays a left-facing pointer (a document page icon with the upper left corner folded down) when you drag a facing-page pointer (a document page icon with both upper corners folded down) to the page on the left of the document spine.

The program displays a right-facing pointer (a document page icon with the upper right corner folded down) when you drag a facing-page pointer to a page on the right of the document spine.

The program displays a single-sided page pointer (an open square) when you drag a single-sided master page to the left or right of the pages along the spine.

4. When you complete the arrangement of the spread, close the Document Layout palette by clicking the close box in the upper left corner of the palette.

Suppress Printout

Purpose

Speeds printing of a document, especially when the document includes pictures.

To suppress printout of a line or a text box

1. Activate the item for which you want to suppress printout.

2. From the Item menu, select Modify (or press ⌘-M).

   The program displays the Line Specifications or Text Box Specifications dialog box.

3. Select the Suppress Printout check box.

4. Click the OK button.

To suppress printout of a picture box

1. Activate the item for which you want to suppress printout.

2. From the Item menu, select Modify (or press ⌘-M).

   The program displays the Picture Specifications dialog box.

3. To suppress printout of the contents of the picture box, but print the frame or background color, select the Suppress Picture Printout check box.

   To suppress printout of the contents of the picture box, the frame, and the background color, select the Suppress Printout check box.

Tabs

Purpose

Sets predefined locations on the text line where the insertion bar moves when you press the Tab key. You can set Left, Center, Right, and Decimal tabs, and you can use space or a fill character (such as a row of periods, or *leader dots*) between tab stops.

In QuarkXPress, tab stops are paragraph-oriented: you set tab stops for a selected paragraph or range of paragraphs, rather than for a single line. Default tabs are left-aligned at intervals of one-half inch.

To set tab stops

1. Select the paragraph(s) for which you want to set tab stops.

2. From the Style menu, select Tabs (or press ⌘-Shift-T).

   The program displays the Paragraph Tabs dialog box and a ruler at the top of the selected text. The ruler displays up to 20 current tab stops for the selected paragraph(s).

3. In the Alignment area, click the button that indicates the type of tab stop you want to set.

4. Click the ruler at the point where you want to place the tab stop.

   or

   Enter the position of the tab in the Position field.

5. To use a fill character (rather than space) between tab stops, enter the character in the Fill Character field.

6. To view the effects of your tab settings without saving them, click the Apply button.

7. To save the tab settings, click the OK button.

To clear tab stops

1. Select the paragraph(s) for which you want to clear tab stops.

2. From the Style menu, select Tabs (or press ⌘-**Shift-T**).

   The program displays the Paragraph Tabs dialog box and a ruler at the top of the selected text. The ruler displays up to 20 current tab stops for the selected paragraph(s).

3. Hold down the **Option** key and click the ruler.

To align tab stops to a character

1. From the Style menu, select Tabs (or press ⌘-**Shift-T**).

   The program displays the Paragraph Tabs dialog box and a ruler at the top of the selected text. The ruler displays up to 20 current tab stops for the selected paragraph(s).

2. From the Alignment pop-up menu, select Align on and enter a character in the Alignment field.

   If you enter a decimal point (**.**) or comma (**,**) tabs align text to the number that precedes the decimal point or comma.

Templates

Purpose

Provides a preformatted QuarkXPress document you can use again and again to create new documents.

To save a document as a template

1. Activate the document you want to save as a template.

2. From the File menu, select Save (or press ⌘-S) or Save As (or press ⌘-S).

   The program displays the Save dialog box.

3. If the document is new, enter a name in the Save current document as field.

4. To designate the document as a template, click the Template button.

5. Click the Save button.

To view a thumbnail of a template's first page

1. From the File menu, select Open.

   The program displays the Open dialog box.

2. To display the names of the available templates, click the Templates button.

3. Select the template you want to view (highlight its name in the scroll list).

4. Select the Template Preview check box.

   The program displays the first page of the selected template.

5. Click the Open button.

Thumbnails

Purpose

Displays miniatures of document pages.

To view a document in thumbnail mode

From the View menu, select Thumbnails.

The program displays the Document Layout palette (the thumbnail view of the document).

To rearrange the order of pages in a document

1. From the View menu, select Thumbnails.

   The program displays the Document Layout palette (the thumbnail view of the document).

2. Click the icon of the page you want to move and drag it to its new location.

   To move several consecutive pages at one time, click the icon of the first page you want to move, hold down the Shift key as you click the last page you want to move, and then drag all the icons to their new location.

3. Release the mouse button.

To print a thumbnail version of a document

You can print thumbnails only when the selected printer is a PostScript printer.

1. From the File menu, select Print.

   The program displays the Print dialog box.

2. Select the Thumbnails check box.

   Thumbnail pages are one-eighth normal size. The specified paper size and document size determine the number of thumbnails that print on one page.

3. Click the OK button.

TIFF/RIFF Files

Purpose

Stores scanned images. TIFF is an acronym for Tag Image Format File. RIFF is an acronym for Raster Image Format File.

To import a TIFF or RIFF file

1. To create the picture box where you want to place the imported graphic, select one of the picture box tools, then drag the mouse pointer to create the box to size. For more information, see *Boxes*.

2. Select the Content tool and activate the picture box.

3. From the File menu, select Get Picture (or press ⌘-E).

   The program displays the Get Picture dialog box.

4. Select the TIFF or RIFF file you want to import and click the Open button.

or

Double-click the name of the TIFF or RIFF file.

To select the display resolution of TIFF and RIFF files

1. From the Edit menu, select Preferences. From the Preferences submenu, select Application.

   The program displays the Application Preferences dialog box.

2. To display imported TIFF and RIFF pictures at 36 dpi (dots per inch), select the Low Resolution TIFF check box.

   To display imported TIFF and RIFF pictures at 72 dpi, deselect the Low Resolution TIFF check box.

To toggle between low and high resolution

1. From the File menu, select Get Picture.

   The program displays the Get Picture dialog box.

2. Hold down the Shift key and click the Open button.

To modify the format of TIFF files you are importing

1. From the File menu, select Get Picture.

   The program displays the Get Picture dialog box.

2. To convert a TIFF grayscale picture to TIFF line art or to convert a TIFF color picture to a TIFF grayscale picture, hold down the Option key and click the Open button.

Note

See also *Colors*, *Halftone Screens*, *Picture Color*, and *Picture Contrast*.

Tiling

Purpose

Breaks documents that are larger than your paper size into sections that fit on one sheet of paper.

To tile a QuarkXPress document

1. From the File menu, select Print.

   The program displays the Print dialog box.

2. In the Tiling area, select Off (the default), Manual, or Auto overlap.

   If you select Manual, specify the size of the individual tile pieces of the document by moving the origin of the document's ruler.

   If you select Auto overlap, the program specifies the size of the individual tile pieces of the document. In the Auto overlap field, enter the amount of empty space between tiles (from 0 to 6 inches).

3. Click the OK button.

4. When you assemble the document, remove the overlap region.

Tool Palette

Purpose

Contains the tools you use to create a QuarkXPress document.

To show (or hide) the Tool palette

From the View menu, select Show (or Hide) Tools. If the Tool palette is open when you quit a QuarkXPress session, the program automatically opens the Tool palette the next time you start QuarkXPress.

To use the Tool palette

When you select a tool by clicking it, the program highlights the tool. The selected tool determines which menus and menu selections are available. For a list of the tools and their functions, see *Palettes* in the QuarkXPress Basics section.

Tool Preferences

Purpose

Enables you to make changes to default settings for the tools on the Tool palette.

To change default settings for the Tool palette

1. From the Edit menu, select Preferences. From the Preferences submenu, select Tools (or double-click one of the tools on the Tool palette).

   The program displays the Tool Preferences dialog box. The dialog box includes a small version of the Tool palette and indicates the tools for which you can change the defaults. If you opened the Tool Preferences dialog box by double-clicking a tool, that tool is selected.

2. To change preferences for the Zoom tool, select the Zoom tool in the dialog box.

   In the View Scale area, enter the minimum and maximum view sizes (from 10 to 400 percent) in the Minimum and Maximum fields. The default Minimum entry is 10 percent. The default Maximum entry is 400 percent.

   In the Increment field, enter the increment (from 10 to 400 percent) that each click of the mouse button changes the zoomed view. The default increment is 25 percent.

3. To change preferences for the Text Box tool, select the Text Box tool in the dialog box.

   To change the default text box specifications, click the Modify button. The program displays the Text Box Specifications dialog box. The specifications you cannot change are dimmed. For information about valid entries in the Text Box Specifications dialog box, see *Modifying Items*.

To change the default frame specifications, click the Frame button. The program displays the Frame Specifications dialog box. For information about valid entries in the Frame Specifications dialog box, see *Frames*.

To change the default runaround specifications, click the Runaround button. The program displays the Runaround Specifications dialog box. For information about valid entries in the Runaround Specifications dialog box, see *Runaround*.

4. To change preferences for the **Rectangular Picture Box**, **Rounded-Corner Rectangular Picture Box**, **Oval Picture Box**, or **Polygon Picture Box** tools, select the tool you want to change.

To change the default picture box specifications, click the Modify button. The program displays the Picture Box Specifications dialog box. The specifications you cannot change are dimmed. For information about valid entries in the Picture Box Specifications dialog box, see *Modifying Items*.

To change the default frame specifications, click the Frame button. The program displays the Frame Specifications dialog box. For information about valid entries in the Picture Box Specifications dialog box, see *Frames*.

To change the default runaround specifications, click the Runaround button. The program displays the Runaround Specifications dialog box. For information about valid entries in the Runaround Specifications dialog box, see *Runaround*.

5. To change preferences for the **Line** or **Orthogonal Line** tools, select the tool you want to change.

To change the default line specifications, click the Modify button. The program displays the Line Specifications dialog box. The specifications you cannot change are dimmed. For information about valid entries in the Line Specifications dialog box, see *Lines*.

To change the default runaround specifications for one of the line tools, click the Runaround button. The program displays the Runaround Specifications dialog box. For information about valid entries in the Runaround Specifications dialog box, see *Runaround*.

Tracking

Purpose

Adjusts the amount of space between a range of selected characters or selected words.

To track by using a dialog box

1. Select the characters you want to track.

2. From the Style menu, select Track.

   The program displays the Track Amount dialog box. If you have not previously tracked any of the selected characters, the value in the Track Amount field is 0 (zero).

3. In the Track Amount field, enter a value from –500 to 500. The measurement unit for manual tracking is .005, or 1/200, *em space*. (In QuarkXPress, an em space is the width of two zeros in the current font.) A negative value decreases the distance between the two characters; a positive value increases the distance.

4. Click the OK button.

Measurements palette method

1. Highlight the characters you want to track.

2. From the View menu, select Show Measurements.

   The program displays the Measurements palette.

3. Enter a value in the Tracking field.

   or

   To decrease or increase tracking in .05-em space increments, click the left or right Tracking arrows.

   To decrease or increase tracking .005-em space increments, hold down the Option key and click the left or right Tracking arrows.

Command Reference

4. To save the tracking values, press **Enter**.

Keyboard method

1. Select the **Content** tool and then select the characters you want to track.

2. To increase tracking in .05-em space increments, press **⌘-Shift-}**.

    To increase tracking in .005-em space increments, press **⌘-Option-Shift-}**.

    To decrease tracking in .05-em space increments, press **⌘-Shift-{**.

    To decrease tracking in .005-em space increments, press **⌘-Option-Shift-{**.

Trapping

Purpose

Prevents white space between two objects of different colors on a printed page.

To specify trapping preferences

1. From the Edit menu, select Preferences. From the Preferences submenu, select Application.

    The program displays the Application Preferences dialog box. You select trapping preferences in the Trap area.

2. From the Auto Method pop-up menu, select Absolute or Proportional.

    If you select Absolute, the program traps using the value in the Auto Amount field (based on the darker of the object color or background color). If you select Proportional, the program traps using a fraction of the value in the Auto Amount field (based on the difference between the darkness, or luminance, of the object color and background color). The program chokes the background color (if the object color is darker) or spreads the object color (if the object color is lighter).

3. In the Auto Amount field, enter the amount of choke or spread the program applies when trapping an object color and a background color that have the relationship specified in the Trap Specifications dialog box.

4. In the Indeterminate field, enter the amount of choke or spread the program applies when trapping an object color and a multicolor background that have the relationship specified in the Trap Specifications dialog box.

5. In the Overprint Limit field, enter a percentage of shade at or above which the color black specified as Auto (or any other color specified as Overprint) in the Trap Specifications dialog box overprints a background color.

6. To make all items overprint a white background, select the Ignore White check box.

To specify trapping values

1. From the Edit menu, select Colors.

   The program displays the Colors dialog box.

2. From the Color scroll list, select the color for which you want to set trapping values.

3. Click the Edit Trap button.

   The program displays the Trap Specifications dialog box for the selected color.

4. From the Background Color scroll list, select one or more background colors for which you want to set a trapping relationship with the selected color.

   The Value column lists the trapping value(s) for the selected color (see step 2) and the color(s) you selected from the Background color list.

5. To trap the selected color according to the program's trapping algorithm, click the Automatic button.

6. To print the selected color on top of the background color(s), click the Overprint button.

7. To specify a custom trapping value, enter a value (from −5 to +5 points in increments of .001 of any measurement system) in the Trap field.

A negative value reduces, or *chokes*, the knockout area of the background color. A positive value increases, or *spreads*, the size of the object with the selected color against the background color.

8. Click the OK button.

Typesetter's Punctuation

Purpose

Converts foot and inch marks to apostrophes and opening and closing quotation marks, and converts double hyphens to em dashes.

To convert punctuation when importing a text file

1. Select the **Content** tool and activate the text box into which you want to import a text file.

2. From the File menu, select Get Text.

   The program displays the Get Text dialog box.

3. Select the text file you want to import.

4. Select the Convert Quotes check box. (The program selects this option by default).

5. Click the Open button.

   The program imports the text file into the text box, converting foot and inch marks to apostrophes and opening and closing quotation marks and converting double hyphens to em dashes.

To use typesetter's punctuation when editing text

To type an opening double quotation mark, press **Option-[**. To type a closing double quotation mark, press **Option-Shift-[**.

To type an opening single quotation mark, press **Option-]**. To type a closing single quotation mark, press **Option-Shift-]**.

To type an em dash, press **Option-Shift-hyphen**.

Typographic Preferences

Purpose

Enables you to specify the placement and appearance of text.

To set typographic preferences

1. From the Edit menu, select Preferences. From the Preferences submenu, select Typographic (or press ⌘**-Option-Y**).

   The program displays the Typographic Preferences dialog box.

2. In the Superscript area, enter values in the Offset, VScale, and HScale fields.

   In the Offset field, enter the distance superscript characters extend above the baseline (from 0 to 100 percent of their font size). The default Offset is 33 percent.

   In the VScale and HScale fields, enter the height and width of superscript characters (from 0 to 100 percent of their font size). The default VScale value is 100 percent.

3. In the Subscript area, enter values in the Offset, VScale, and HScale fields.

   In the Offset field, enter the distance subscript characters extend below the baseline (from 0 to 100 percent of their font size). The default Offset value is 33 percent.

   In the VScale and HScale fields, enter the height and width of subscript characters. The default VScale value is 100 percent.

4. In the Small Caps area, enter the height and width of small caps characters in the VScale and HScale fields. The default values are 75 percent.

5. In the Superior area, enter the height and width of superior characters in the VScale and HScale fields. The default values are 50 percent.

6. In the Baseline Grid area, enter values in the Start and Increment fields.

   In the Start field, enter the distance from the top of the page to the first line of the grid. The default Start value is 0.5 inches.

   In the Increment field, enter the interval (from 5 to 144 points in increments of .001 point) between baselines. The default Increment value is 12 points.

7. In the Auto Leading field, enter the amount of leading in paragraphs that have the Auto setting.

   To place the baseline of a line of text that is below an obstruction in a column or box according to its leading value, select the Maintain Leading check box.

8. To use kerning tables when the font is as large as the size specified in the Auto Kern Above field, select the Auto Kern Above check box.

   To change the value in the Auto Kern Above field, enter a font size (from 2 to 720 points in increments of .001 of any measurement system).

9. From the Character Widths pop-up menu, select Fractional or Integral spacing for displayed and printed characters. If you are using a LaserWriter or PostScript printer, select Fractional (the default). If you are using an ImageWriter or other dot-matrix printer, select Integral.

10. In the Leading Mode pop-up menu, select Typesetting or Word Processing. Typesetting mode (the default) measures leading from the baseline of a line of text to the baseline immediately above it. Word processing mode measures leading from the top of the ascent on a line of text to the top of the ascent on the line below it.

11. In the Flex Space Width field, enter the width of a flexible space (from 0 percent to 400 percent of a normal word space). For more information, see the Using QuarkXPress manual.

12. From the Ligatures pop-up menu, select whether the program automatically uses the ligatures contained in a font. In the Ligatures field, enter the kerning or

tracking value above which the program does not combine characters into ligatures. For more information, see the Using QuarkXPress manual.

13. Click the OK button.

Views

Purpose

Provides predefined ways to view the document on-screen and enables you to create custom views.

To use a predefined view

From the View menu, select one of the following commands:

Command	*Effect*
Fit in Window (or press ⌘-0)	Displays an entire page in the document window. To display an entire spread, hold down the Option key as you select Fit in Window.
50 percent	Displays a document page at 50 percent of its normal size.
75 percent	Displays a document page at 75 percent of its normal size.
Actual Size (or press ⌘-1)	Displays a document page at its normal size.
200 percent	Displays a document page at 200 percent of its normal size.
Thumbnails	Displays a document page at one eighth of its normal size.

To use a custom view

1. In the View Percent field (in the lower left corner of the document window), enter a percentage (from 10 to 400 percent in .1-percent increments) of the normal document size.

2. To switch to this view, press Enter or click the document.

Tool palette method

1. Select the Zoom tool and activate the document.

2. To reduce the document in predefined increments, hold down the Option key and click the document with the Zoom tool.

   To select part of the document on which to zoom in, drag the Zoom tool to highlight the area.

Word Processing

Purpose

Enables you to enter, edit, move, copy, and delete text within QuarkXPress.

To use word processing

1. Select the Content tool and activate the text box in which you want to use word processing.

2. Position the insertion bar where you want to begin word processing and click the mouse button.

3. To enter text, type the text.

4. To edit text, see *Keyboard Shortcuts*.

5. To move or copy text, drag the mouse to select (highlight) the text and select Cut (⌘-X) or Copy (⌘-C) from the Edit menu. Then, position the insertion bar where you want to place the text and select Paste (⌘-V) from the Edit menu.

6. To delete text, drag the mouse to select (highlight) the text and press Del.

XPress Tags

Purpose

Saves QuarkXPress file-formatting information in an ASCII text file.

XPress Tag examples

The following list is only a brief sample of XPress Tags.

XPress Tag	Effect
<P>	Plain
<B>	Bold
<I>	Italic
<U>	Underline
<K>	All Caps
<H>	Small Caps
<*L>	Left-aligned
<*C>	Centered
<*R>	Right-aligned
<*J>	Justified

For a complete list of XPress Tags, see the QuarkXPress Reference manual.

To use XPress Tags within QuarkXPress

1. From the File menu, select Save Text.

   The program displays the Save Text dialog box.

2. From the Format pop-up menu, select XPress Tags. If XPress Tags is not available on the pop-up menu, place the XPress Tags Xtension in the QuarkXPress folder and restart the program.

3. Enter the XPress Tags in the text.

4. From the File menu, select Save Text .

   The program displays the Save Text dialog box.

5. Save the file as an ASCII file.

To use XPress Tags within another program

1. Position the insertion bar before the text to which you want to apply the XPress Tag(s). To specify a format for a paragraph, position the insertion bar at the beginning of the paragraph.

2. Enter the XPress Tag code(s). You can type more than one XPress Tag code within the angle brackets (< and >).
3. Save the file as an ASCII file.

Xtensions

Purpose

Adds additional capabilities to QuarkXPress. To obtain a list of Xtensions, write to Quark at the following address:

> Quark, Inc.
> 300 South Jackson, Suite 100
> Denver, CO 80209

To use an Xtension

Before starting a session with QuarkXPress, place the Xtension in the same folder as the QuarkXPress folder.

When QuarkXPress starts, it treats any Xtension in its folder as if it were part of the program itself.

Index

A

activating items, 8
alignment
  boxes, anchored, 93
  items, 120-121
  paragraph
    horizontal, 9
    modifying, 93
    vertical, 10
Alignment command, 9
anchoring
  boxes, 12
    alignment, 93
    modifying, 12
    moving, 12
  lines, 12
  rules, 10-11
appending
  color palettes, 13
  styles, 13, 54
Application Preferences, 14-16
  default settings, 32
Apply button, 16
applying, 16
Arrow pointer, 82
arrows, 82-83
asbolute leading, 78
attributes
  characters, 32
  text, 40-42

B

background color, 109
Balloon Help, 60
baseline
  grid, 17
  shifting characters relative to, 18
  text, locking, 17
Baseline Shift command, 18
bleeds, 18
borders, *see* frames
boxes
  anchored, 12
    alignment, 93
    modifying, 12
    moving, 12
  check, 4
  frames, 47-48
  locking, 87
  picture, 19-20, 30, 34
  text, 20, 30, 34, 67-69, 78, 86
  unlocking, 88
buttons, 4-5

C

caps, 65-66
character strings, 92-93
characters
  aligning tabs to, 128
  attributes, 32
  nonprinting, searching and
    replacing, 39
  shifting relative to baseline, 18
  special, 121-123
check boxes, 4
Check Spelling command, 21-23
checking spelling, 21-23
clicking, 2
Clipboard, 30
closing documents, 8, 99-100
Color command, 45, 109
color palette
  adding a color, 13
  default settings, 32
  deleting a color, 26
color wheel, 24
colors
  applying, 109
  brightness, 24
  defining, 24
  duplicating, 25
  editing, 25
  FOCOLTONE, 24
  grid lines, 14
  guides, 57
  lines, 83-84
  margins, 14
  palette, 26
  PANTONE, 24
  picture, 108-109
  process, 24, 114-115
  rulers, 14, 57
  rules, 11
  separations, 26
  shading, 45
  spot, 115, 123-124
  text, 26, 45
  TRUMATCH, 24
Colors command, 13, 24-25, 32,
  114, 137

columns
  guides, 58
    master page, 28, 90
  number
    in new documents, 27
    in text box, 27, 92
  space between, 94
command buttons, 4-5
commands, selecting from menus, 3
Constrain command, 28
constraining, 28
Content tool, 7
"continued from page..." message, 29
"continued on page..." message, 29
Continuous Apply mode, 16
contrast, 109-111
Copy command, 12, 30
copying
  boxes, 30
  formats, 108
  lines, 83
  text, 30
crop marks, 113
Cut command, 12-13, 34, 66

D

default settings, 30
  Application Preferences, 32
  character attributes, 32
  character spacing, 33
  color palette, 32
  General Preferences, 31
  hyphenation, 33
  paragraph formats, 32
  Tool palette, 133-134
  Tool Preferences, 31
  Typographic Preferences, 31
  word spacing, 33
Delete command, 34, 83
deleting
  from a group, 34
  from libraries, 81
  keyboard shortcuts, 35
  lines, 34, 83
  master page, 91
  pages, 34
  picture boxes, 34
  pictures, 34
  text, 34
  text boxes, 34
dialog boxes, 3
  fields, 4
  keyboard shortcuts, 72
Display command, 101
Document Layout palette, 5

Document Setup command, 105
document windows, 8
documents
  checking spelling, 23
  columns, 27
  opening and closing, 8, 99-100
double-clicking, 2
dragging mouse, 2
drop caps, 65-66
Duplicate command, 36, 83
duplicating, 83

E–F

ellipsis (...), 3
Endpoints, 84
exporting text, 37

fields, 4
filters, 13
Find/Change command, 38-39
FOCOLTONE color, 24
Font command, 42
Font Usage command, 46-47
fonts
  changing, 42, 46
  character strings, 93
  kerning tables, 69
  multiple changes, 46
  size, 43
  style, 44
  usage, 46
formats, 106-108
Formats command, 17, 64, 106-107
Frame command, 48
frames, 47-48

G

General Preferences, 31, 49
Get Picture command, 51, 108, 130
Get Text command, 53
graphics
  importing, 51
  previewing, 52
  see also pictures
greeking, 54-55
grid lines
  baseline, 17
  color, 14
groups, 55
  deleting from, 34
  modifying, 55
  rotating, 117
  ungrouping, 56
guides
  background, 57
  colors, 57

column, 58
foreground, 57
hiding, 56
margin, 88
snapping to, 57
vertical, 58

H

H&Js command, 61
Hairline, 83
halftone screens, 58-60
handles, 8, 82
hanging indents, 65
Help, 60-61
Hide Guides command, 56
Hide Rulers command, 56
Hide Tools command, 132
High Contrast command, 111
highlighting text, 8
horizontal scale, 45
Horizontal Scale command, 45
hyphenation, 61-63
Hyphenation Exceptions
  command, 63

I

importing
  current version of file, 52
  RIFF files, 130
  TIFF files, 130
  graphics, 51-52
  Microsoft Word documents, 54
  PICT files, 108
  text, 53
incremental leading, 78
indents, 64-65
initial caps, 65-66
Item tool, 7
items
  activating, 8
  aligning, 120-121
  commands, keyboard shortcuts,
    75-76
  distributing, 120-121
  duplicating, 36
    Step and Repeat, 36
  handles, 8
  modifying, 93, 97
  multiple grouping, 55
  repositioning, 92
  resizing, 92
  rotating, 92
  text, runaround, 118-119
  ungrouping, 56

J–K

justification, 61-62
  paragraph, 9-10

Kern command, 68
kerning
  automatic, 67
  keyboard shortcuts, 68
  manual, 68
  tables, 67, 69
Kerning Table Edit command, 69
key combinations, 1
keyboard shortcuts
  alignment, 9
  deleting, 35
  dialog boxes, 72
  font style, 44
  fonts, 43
  item commands, 75-76
  kerning, 68
  leading, 78
  lines, 85
  measurement commands, 77
  menu commands, 70-72
  picture commands, 76-77
  text commands, 73-75
  Tool palette, 77
  tracking, 136

L

labels, library entries, 81
leading
  asbolute, 78
  incremental, 78
  keyboard shortcuts, 78
  paragraph, 92
  paragraph format, 79
  text boxes, 78
Leading command, 78
leading mode, 79
Left Point, 84
libraries, 79
  adding, 80
  creating, 80
  deleting from, 81
  entries
    labeling, 81
    placing into document pages,
      81
  opening, 80
  saving after entries, 81
Library command, 80
Library palette, 6
Line tools, 7
lines
  anchored, 12
  arrows, 83
  colors, 83-84

copying, 83
cutting, 83
deleting, 34, 83
drawing, 82
duplicating, 83
Endpoints, 84
handles, 82
keyboard shortcuts, 85
Left Point, 84
length, 82
locked, 87-88
Midpoint, 84
modifying, 83
moving, 82
nonprinting, 56
pasting, 83
Right Point, 84
rotating, 82
Step and Repeat, 83
suppressing printing, 126
thickness, 83
unlocking, 88
linking, 86-87
Linking tool, 7
Lock command, 87
locking
boxes, 87
lines, 87-88
unlocking, 88

M

margins
color, 14
guides, 88
master page, 90
setting, 88
Master Guides command, 28, 58
master pages
changes, controlling, 91
checking spelling, 23
column guides, 28, 90
creating, 89
deleting, 91
format, 91
margins, 90
naming, 90
order, 90
Measurement palette, 6, 92
measurement units, 49-50
keyboard shortcuts, 77
rulers, 57
menu bar, 3
menus
commands, keyboard shortcuts, 70-72
menu bar, 3
pop-up, 4
selecting, 3
submenus, 3

Midpoint, 84
Modify command, 10-12, 83, 93
modifying
alignment, paragraphs, 93
boxes
anchored, 12
picture, 20
text, 20
groups, 55
indents, paragraph, 64
items, 93, 97
kerning tables, 69
leading, paragraphs, 92
lines, 83
picture boxes, 95-96
text boxes, 93-95
mouse, 2-3
Move command, 97-98
Mover pointer, 82
moving, 97-98
boxes, anchored, 12
lines, 82
locked, 88
pages, 97-98
picture box, 98
text boxes, 98

N-O

New command, 27, 58, 88
Normal Contrast command, 111
Normal Screens command, 59
nudging, 98

opening
documents, 8, 99-100
libraries, 80
option buttons, 4
Orthogonal Line tool, 7
Other Contrast command, 110
Other Screen command, 59
Oval Picture Box tool, 7
overflow text, 87

P

page setup
ImageWriter printer, 104
PostScript printer, 102-104
Page Setup command, 102-104
page size, 105
pages
deleting, 34
moving, 97-98
numbering, 100-101
order, 129
palettes, 5
color
adding to, 13
default settings, 32
deleting from, 26

Document Layout, 5
Library, 6
Measurement, 6, 92
Tool, 6, 132
  hiding, 132
  keyboard shortcuts, 77
PANTONE colors, 24
paragraphs
  alignment
    horizontal, 9
    modifying, 93
    vertical, 10
  attributes, 106-107
  formats, 32, 106-108
  indents, 64
  justification, 9-10
  leading, 79, 92
pasting, 80, 83
PICT files, 108
Picture Box tool, 7
picture boxes, 8, 19
  circular, 20
  copying, 30
  deleting, 34
  graphics, 51
  modifying, 20, 95-96
  moving, 98
  nudging, 98
  resizing, 116-117
  rotating, 96, 117
  size, 96
  square, 20
  suppressing printing, 126
pictures
  color, 108-109
  commands, keyboard shortcuts, 76-77
  contrast, 109-111
  deleting, 34
  posterizing, 111
  slanting, *see* skewing
pointers, 3
  Arrow, 82
  Mover, 82
  Resizing, 82
Polygon tool, 7
pop-up menus, 4
Posterized command, 111
preferences
  Application, 14-16
  default settings, 31-32
  General, 49
  Tool, 133
  Typographic, 139-140
Preferences command, 14, 17, 31, 47
previewing
  graphics, 52
  hyphenation, 63
Print command, 112

printers, 102-104
printing
  color separations, 26
  cover pages, 112
  crop marks, 113
  monitoring progress, 114
  preparation, 112
  registration marks, 113-115
  thumbnails, 130
process color, 24, 114-115

R

raised cap, 66
Rectangular Picture Box tool, 7
redrawing, 15
registration marks, 113-115
resizing
  items, 92
  picture boxes, 116-117
  text boxes, 116-117
  text characters, 116
Resizing pointer, 82
RIFF files, 130-131
Right Point, 84
rotating
  groups, 117
  items, 92
  lines, 82
  picture boxes, 96, 117
  text boxes, 94, 117
Rotation tool, 7
Rounded-Corner Rectangluar Picture Box tool, 7
rulers
  colors, 14, 57
  hiding, 56
  measurement units, 57
  nonprinting, 56
rules, 10-11
Rules command, 10
runaround, 118
Runaround command, 118

S

Save command, 129
Save Text command, 37
scaling, 45
screens
  halftone, 58-60
  redrawing, 15
  resolution, 52
scrolling, 15
search and replace, 37
searching and replacing
  character, nonprinting, 39
  text, 38-42
  wildcards, 39

Section command, 101
service bureaus, 119
shading, 45
  lines, 84
Show Document command, 125
Show Document Layout command, 89
Show Guides command, 56
Show Invisibles command, 121
Show Rulers command, 56
Show Tools command, 132
Size command, 43
skewing, 120
Snap Distance, 56-57
Snap to Guides command, 56-57
Space/Align command, 120
spacing, 33
special characters, 121-123
spelling, *see* checking spelling
spot color, 123-124
spreads, 124-126
Step and Repeat command, 36, 83
Style Sheets command, 13, 32
styles
  appending, 13
  font, 93
  importing, 54
submenu indicator, 3
submenus, 3
Suggested Hyphenation command, 63
suppressing
  line, 126
  printing, 126
suspect words, 23

T

tables, kerning, 67
tabs, 127-128
Tabs command, 127
templates, 128-129
text
  attributes, 40-42
  characters, 116
  color, 26, 45
  commands, keyboard shortcuts, 73-75
  copying, 30
  deleting, 34
  entering, 142
  exporting, 37
  highlighting, 8
  horizontal scale, 45
  importing, 53
  lines, anchored to, 12
  overflow, 87
  retrieving, 53
  runaround, 118-119
  searching and replacing, 38-39
Text Box tool, 7
text boxes, 8, 20, 93-95
  copying, 30
  deleting, 34
  leading, 78
  linking, 86
  modifying, 20
  moving, 98
  number of columns, 27, 92
  resizing, 116-117
  rotating, 94, 117
  size, 94
  suppressing printing, 126
thumbnails, 129-130
Thumbnails command, 129
TIFF files
  converting, 52
  display resolution, 131
  format, modifying, 131
  importing, 130
  screen resolution, 52
tiling, 132
Tool palette, 6, 132
  default settings, 133-134
  hiding, 132
  keyboard shortcuts, 77
Tool preferences, 31, 133
Tools, 7
Track command, 135
tracking
  character strings, 92
  keyboard shortcuts, 136
  with dialog box, 135
trapping, 136-137
TRUMATCH color, 24
Type Style command, 44
type style, *see* fonts
typesetters' punctuation, 138
Typographic Preferences, 31, 139-140

U–Z

Unconstrain command, 28
Unlinking tool, 7
Unlock command, 88

vertical guides, 58
viewing documents, 141-142

wildcards, 39
windows, 8
word processing, 142
word wrap, *see* runaround

XPress Tags, 143
Xtensions, 144

Zoom tool, 7